THIS BOOK BELONGS TO

_____

START DATE

_____

SHE READS TRUTH

@SHEREADSTRUTH

Download the
She Reads Truth app,
available for iOS
and Android

Subscribe to the
She Reads Truth podcast

SHEREADSTRUTH.COM

EXECUTIVE

FOUNDER/CHIEF EXECUTIVE OFFICER
Raechel Myers

CO-FOUNDER/CHIEF CONTENT OFFICER
Amanda Bible Williams

CHIEF OPERATING OFFICER
Ryan Myers

EXECUTIVE ASSISTANT
Sarah Andereck

EDITORIAL

EDITORIAL DIRECTOR
Jessica Lamb

CONTENT EDITOR
Kara Gause

ASSOCIATE EDITORS
Bailey Gillespie
Tameshia Williams

EDITORIAL ASSISTANT
Hannah Little

CREATIVE

CREATIVE DIRECTOR
Jeremy Mitchell

LEAD DESIGNER
Kelsea Allen

DESIGNERS
Abbey Benson
Davis DeLisi
Annie Glover

MARKETING

MARKETING DIRECTOR
Krista Juline Williams

MARKETING MANAGER
Katie Matuska Pierce

SOCIAL MEDIA MANAGER
Ansley Rushing

COMMUNITY SUPPORT SPECIALIST
Margot Williams

SHIPPING & LOGISTICS

LOGISTICS MANAGER
Lauren Gloyne

SHIPPING MANAGER
Sydney Bess

CUSTOMER SUPPORT SPECIALIST
Katy McKnight

FULFILLMENT SPECIALISTS
Abigail Achord
Cait Baggerman

SUBSCRIPTION INQUIRIES
orders@shereadstruth.com

CONTRIBUTORS

PHOTOGRAPHY
Rachel Dwyer (6, 46, 76, 106, 136)
Madeline Mullenbach (22, 30, 40, 56,
60, 70, 80, 88, 100, 114, 126, 140)

SHE READS TRUTH™

© 2021 by She Reads Truth, LLC

All rights reserved.

All photography used by permission.

ISBN 978-1-952670-12-1

1 2 3 4 5 6 7 8 9 10

All Scripture is taken from the Christian Standard Bible®. Copyright © 2020 by Holman Bible Publishers. Used by permission. Christian Standard Bible® and CSB® are federally registered trademarks of Holman Bible Publishers.

Research support provided by Logos Bible Software™. Learn more at logos.com.

Though the dates and locations in this book have been carefully researched, scholars disagree on the dating and locations of many biblical events.

This book was printed offset in Nashville, Tennessee, on 70# Lynx Opaque. Cover is 100# Cougar Opaque with a soft touch lamination.

JOSHUA

REMEMBER & PROCLAIM

Only God's faithfulness holds fast—
in the everyday and the impossible.

Amanda

Amanda Bible Williams
CO-FOUNDER & CHIEF
CONTENT OFFICER

"I don't know how you did a year of this," she texted. "I'm three weeks in, and I'm heartbroken and exhausted." My friend was in the NICU with her brand new baby girl, a precious early bird who was growing stronger by the day but still weeks, possibly months, from going home.

It isn't hard to coax my memory back there—to the fluorescent lights of hospital hallways, to days and nights that bleed together into one endless battle to reach the exit door. I remember it vividly, including the feeling she described: to keep going is imperative, but it truly feels impossible.

But it doesn't take a loved one in the hospital for us to feel this way, does it? Life on this side of heaven is too often marked by heartbreaking moments and exhausting seasons where it's all we can do to put one foot in front of the other. We don't need extreme circumstances to be aware of our frailty and certainly not of our overwhelm. I felt that tightening in my own chest just this morning under the weight of the day's demands. So how in this beautiful, broken world do we—those who believe in the one true God and follow His Son, Jesus—respond when we can't take another step?

We remember. We remember what God has done, what He is doing, and what He says He will do.

Our team has a communication channel we call "Keep Going." It's the place where we put stories and notes of encouragement from you, our community, so we can remember and celebrate God's work among us. Because if we've learned one thing from being in the Word of God every day, it's this: His faithfulness is our fuel. Our best efforts, plans, and intentions are fine, but they're also frail. Only God's faithfulness holds fast—in the everyday and the impossible. This is Joshua's story and ours.

This Joshua Study Book is designed to continually lift our gaze to God. The film images of the Holy Land allow us to see where God faithfully pursued, protected, and provided for His people in real time and space, just as He's doing even now. The weekly reflections challenge us to remember and proclaim God's faithfulness in our own lives, and the theological extras help us connect this Old Testament account with the whole of Scripture. The "Joshua & Jesus" extra on page 118 makes me throw my hands up in worship!

Friends, this book is our history, and it is deeply important. The physical battles and earthly victories of God's people in this historical account foreshadow the spiritual battle and eternal victory won for us in the life, death, and resurrection of Jesus. The inheritance of the promised land is but a glimpse of our eternal inheritance secured in Christ—not by our goodness, but by His.

As you read these pages, pause and remember God's faithfulness to you. Remember and proclaim. Then rejoice and keep going, for the Lord your God goes with you wherever you go.

At She Reads Truth, we believe in pairing the inherently beautiful Word of God with the aesthetic beauty it deserves. Each of our resources is thoughtfully and artfully designed to highlight the beauty, goodness, and truth of Scripture in a way that reflects the themes of each curated reading plan.

Throughout the book of Joshua, stones were used as a visual aid to memorialize fulfilled promises and remember God's faithfulness. Throughout this Study Book, you'll find photographs of modern stone arrangements to remind us of God's faithfulness to His people.

We also incorporated scanned mulberry paper into our design. The textured and semi-translucent paper is made with pulp from the mulberry tree, which traditionally symbolizes abundance. We used it in this book and on the cover as a visual representation of both the promises of God and the physical land Israel claims in the narrative, a land "flowing with milk and honey."

We chose to include photography taken by Madeline Mullenbach in this book. Each image was shot on film in Israel. We've noted the modern-day location and tribal territory for each image to help connect the regions and locations in our reading to the actual places where these events occurred.

HOW TO USE THIS BOOK

She Reads Truth is a community of women dedicated to reading the Word of God every day. The Bible is living and active, and we confidently hold it higher than anything we can do or say.

READ & REFLECT

This **Joshua** Study Book focuses primarily on Scripture, with bonus resources to facilitate deeper engagement with God's Word.

SCRIPTURE READING

Designed for a Monday start, this Study Book presents the book of Joshua in daily readings, with supplemental passages for additional context.

REFLECTION

Each week features space for notes and prompts for reflection.

COMMUNITY & CONVERSATION

Join women from Indio, CA, to Italy as they read with you!

 ### SHE READS TRUTH APP

Devotionals corresponding to each daily reading can be found in the **Joshua** reading plan on the She Reads Truth app. You can also participate in community discussions, download free lock screens for Weekly Truth memorization, and more.

GRACE DAY

Use Saturdays to catch up on your reading, pray, and rest in the presence of the Lord.

WEEKLY TRUTH

Sundays are set aside for Scripture memorization.

EXTRAS

This book features additional tools to help you gain a deeper understanding of the text.

See a complete list of extras on the following pages.

 SHEREADSTRUTH.COM

All of our reading plans and devotionals are also available at SheReadsTruth.com. Invite your family, friends, and neighbors to read along with you!

 SHE READS TRUTH PODCAST

Join our She Reads Truth founders and their guests each Monday as they open their Bibles and talk about the beauty, goodness, and truth they find there. Subscribe to the podcast so you don't miss conversations about the current commmunity reading plan.

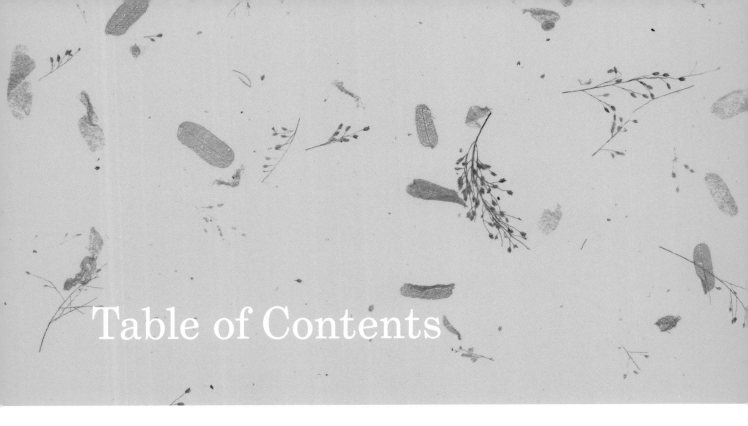

Table of Contents

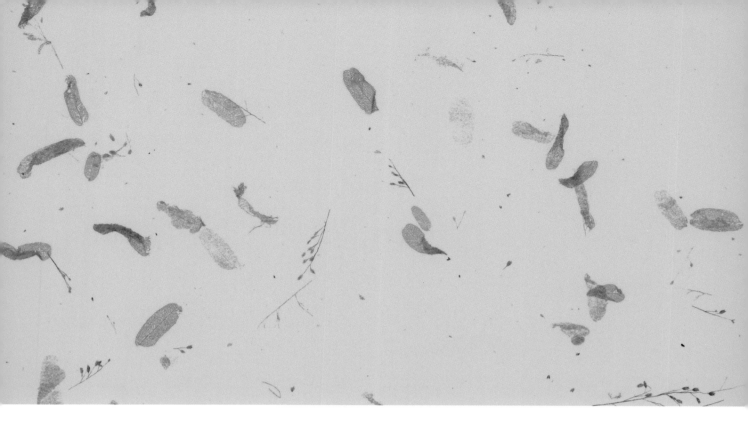

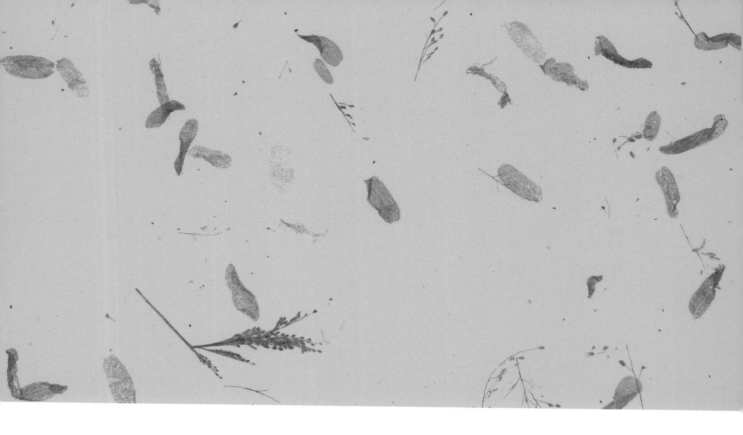

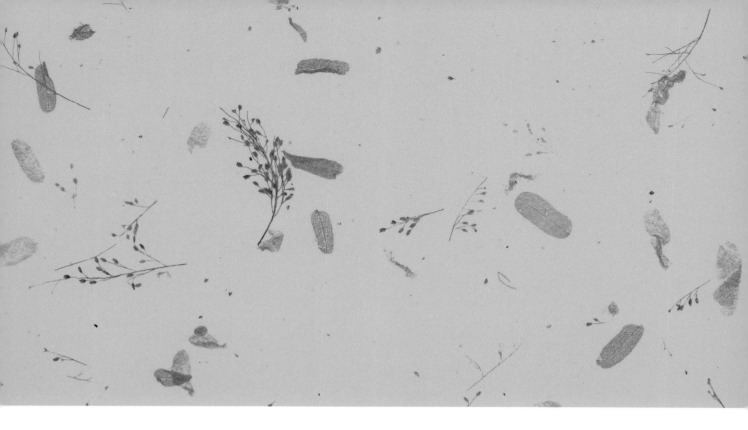

She Reads Joshua

ON THE TIMELINE

Joshua is the first of the Historical Books in the Old Testament. These events took place in the time between Moses's death and Joshua's, beginning with God telling Joshua to lead the people of Israel into the long-awaited promised land. Israel first appeared in the land west of the Jordan River around 1406 BC, and Joshua died after the tribal allotments of Israel, around 1380 BC.

A LITTLE BACKGROUND

The author of the book of Joshua is not identified. If Joshua himself did not originally write the book that bears his name, someone who knew him well likely did. There are a number of references throughout Joshua that suggest final editing of the book after his lifetime. These include the death of Joshua and descriptions of memorials or names "still there today" (Jos 4:9; 10:27; 15:63; 23:8).

MESSAGE & PURPOSE

Chapter 1 establishes Joshua as Israel's divinely appointed leader and successor to Moses. God addressed Joshua directly, promising him the land that He promised to Moses (Dt 34:4), as well as His divine presence (Jos 1:3–5). The commands to "be strong and very courageous" (Jos 1:6–7, 9) define the mission of Joshua.

The book of Joshua is a record of God's fulfillment of His part of the renewed covenant in Deuteronomy. God gave Israel victories, but each victory required a step of faith. God's provision for the people as their leader and guide was recorded in this book and recounted to later generations.

GIVE THANKS FOR THE BOOK OF JOSHUA

The book of Joshua describes the history of the generation of Israel who crossed the Jordan River and entered the promised land of Canaan. Joshua led God's people to defeat those who opposed them, and their battles have a place among the greatest stories of faith in the Old Testament. God's holiness and saving acts are evident throughout the book, serving as a reminder of His faithfulness to His covenant and His people. By God's grace alone, the nation was able to occupy the land, receive their inheritance, and worship their God.

KEY VERSE

"Haven't I commanded you: be strong and courageous? Do not be afraid or discouraged, for the LORD your God is with you wherever you go."

JOSHUA 1:9

HISTORICAL NARRATIVE IN THE BIBLE

The twelve Historical Books in the Old Testament form the true account of God's relationship with the people of Israel, from their entry into the promised land to their exile and return. Here are some helpful tips to remember when reading historical narrative in the Bible.

Historical narrative is also theological history, written to show how God works in and through historical events. Historical narrative in the Bible records true events but was written to do more than just document history.

Biblical narrative is often descriptive rather than prescriptive. Examples are not always positive or meant to be followed.

Our social norms are different from those we encounter in the Bible. God spoke into culture as it existed.

God's revelation is gradual. Since we have the complete Old and New Testaments, we benefit from knowledge about certain aspects of God's plan that the people we read about in the Old Testament did not.

The Bible was written by people living in the middle of redemption history. What they wrote was often selected to explain the circumstances God's people were experiencing in their own day.

People in the Bible are complex and rarely fall into neat categories of "good" and "bad." Jesus is the only one who is truly good.

God worked through broken, sinful people in the Bible, and He still does.

The book of Joshua is part of the Old Testament story of Israel, the nation set apart by God to bless the world. Israel's story is part of the grand narrative of Scripture. Below is a summary of that story.

THE GARDEN OF EDEN

THE PATRIARCHS

THE EXODUS AND THE LAW

God created and blessed the world. He gave the first humans, Adam and Eve, a mission to carry out His purpose for creation beyond Eden throughout the entire world. But when Adam and Eve sinned and failed to carry out that purpose, God promised to send a Savior to restore His plan for all creation.

God called Abraham to leave his home and follow Him to the land of Canaan. He made a covenant with Abraham, promising to position him as the father of a great nation, give him Canaan as an inheritance, and bless the world through the offspring of his son, Isaac. Abraham's grandson Jacob, also called Israel, had twelve sons whose descendants established the twelve tribes of Israel. These descendants became enslaved in Egypt.

God worked through Moses to bring the Israelites out of slavery in Egypt. At Mount Sinai, God made a covenant with the people of Israel, setting them apart as His chosen people in order to make His name known among all other nations. He also gave them the law, the standard by which they were to live and worship. But when the Israelites scouted the land of Canaan that God promised to give them, they were afraid and refused to enter. Because of their disobedience, God made the Israelites wander in the wilderness for forty years until the disobedient generation died.

THE NEW CREATION

THE NATION OF ISRAEL

JESUS AND HIS CHURCH

THE BOOK OF JOSHUA

Under Joshua, the Israelites entered the promised land and began to displace the people living there. Capturing the promised land was a physical act for a spiritual purpose, reclaiming what ultimately already belonged to God as a step in redeeming the entire earth for His purpose and glory.

When Joshua died, the people turned from God, and their sin led to cycles of judgment and deliverance. Eventually, Israel cried out for a king. But after just three kings, the nation split and a series of mostly wicked kings ruled the two kingdoms until Israel, the northern kingdom, and Judah, the southern kingdom, were taken into exile by foreign powers. Through the prophets, God promised He would send an eternal King who would make a new people and restore God's blessing to the entire world.

The four Gospels announce that Jesus's life, death, and resurrection are the fulfillment of God's promise to send a new King and Savior, who would restore God's people and creation to Him. Jesus commissioned His followers to share the good news of His arrival with the nations. Jesus then sent the Holy Spirit to equip His people in carrying out His purposes and message throughout the world. This remains the mission of the Church today.

The world will one day be redeemed from the curse of sin and death. At the end of history, the whole earth will be made new, and the kingdom of this world will fully become the kingdom of God. On that day, "the earth will be filled with the knowledge of the LORD's glory" (Habakkuk 2:14).

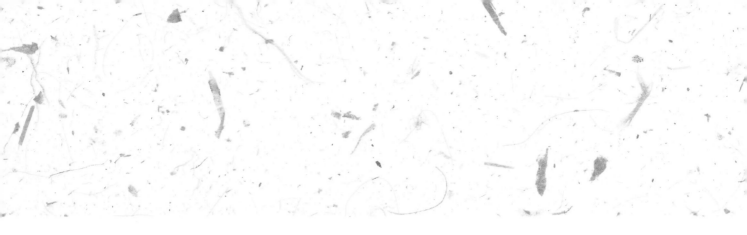

Moments of Remembrance

Remembrance is a key practice in the lives of God's people. The Lord confirmed and renewed His covenant promises throughout Scripture, and on occasion, God commanded the nation of Israel to reflect on their history and remember His wondrous works (Dt 6:10–25; 8). **When we intentionally stop and remember what God has done, we learn to see His faithfulness in the past and present, and we learn to trust Him with our futures.**

Joshua's Calling

JOSHUA 1

Memorial Stones

JOSHUA 4

Throughout the book of Joshua, we'll encounter many moments where the people of God stopped to remember God and His covenant with them. Each of these moments of remembrance will be marked with a symbol in the margins as you read. A summary of each is listed on the following pages.

Each week, you'll have the opportunity to reflect on God's presence and His work in your life, then record those reflections as your own stories of remembrance.

After Moses died, God appointed Joshua as Moses's successor to lead the Israelites across the Jordan River (Dt 31:3). He promised to be with Joshua at every turn—to never leave him or abandon him, just as He had faithfully guided and been with Moses (Jos 1:1–5). Equipped with the promise of God's presence, Joshua told the leaders of the people to gather their things and prepare to enter the long-awaited promised land (Gn 15:18–21; Jos 1:10–11).

When God miraculously dried up the Jordan River, Joshua commanded twelve men—representing the twelve tribes of Israel—to retrieve a stone from the riverbed (Gn 17:20; Jos 4:4–5). Eventually, Joshua set these stones at Gilgal as a sign to future generations to remember the story of God's power and provision (Jos 4:6–7). Not only had the Lord parted the Red Sea so Moses could deliver the Israelites from slavery, but He once again delivered them from destruction by cutting off the Jordan in front of the ark of the covenant (Ex 14:21–23; Jos 4:19–24).

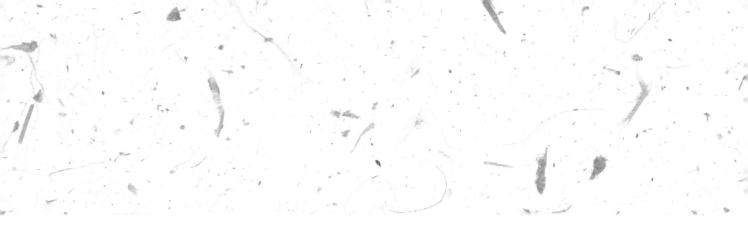

Consecration at Gilgal

JOSHUA 5:1-9

  ③

Safely on the other side of the Jordan, Joshua gathered the people and circumcised all the Israelite men who were born in the wilderness. Circumcision was a sign of the covenant God made with Abraham that He would make him the father of many nations. It was a reminder that Israel's entire bloodline belonged to the Lord (Gn 17:1–8). God did not abandon His covenant with Abraham, and He would not abandon the Israelites now. Despite their faithless wandering, He proved His unwavering commitment to the next generation by this act of consecration (Jos 5:1–9).

Passover Feast

JOSHUA 5:10-12

④

After the men had healed at Gilgal, Joshua and the Israelites celebrated their first Passover in the land promised to Abraham's descendants (Gn 15:18; Ex 3:17; 33:1–3; Jos 5:10–12). Passover, or the Festival of Unleavened Bread, was first established as a way for Israel to remember how God allowed the tenth plague to pass over their doors in Egypt (Ex 12:1–28). By continuing to observe this ceremony, the Israelites remembered God's mercy (Ex 12:25).

Worship at Mount Ebal

JOSHUA 8:30-35

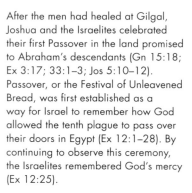 ⑤

After a season of difficult battles, Joshua constructed an altar to worship the Lord on Mount Ebal (Jos 8:30–33). Joshua built this altar just as Moses commanded: from uncut stones to remind Israel of their heritage (Dt 27:1–8). The people gathered and brought the ark of the covenant to the base of the mountain, where Joshua read the law of Moses to the people to remind them of God's instructions for life and worship (Jos 8:30–35).

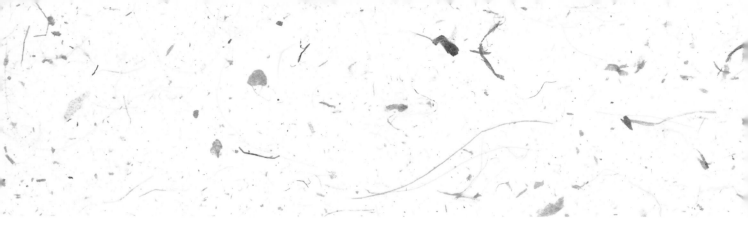

Cities of Refuge

JOSHUA 20

Monument Along the Jordan

JOSHUA 22:9–34

Covenant Renewal

JOSHUA 24:14–28

 6 **7** **8**

Joshua and the people of Israel set apart certain cities in the promised land to serve as safe havens for people who unintentionally took a life (Nm 35:6, 8; Jos 20). The cities not only served as places of refuge, but they also reminded the people that their God was a God of mercy and compassion.

When the tribes of Reuben, Gad, and the eastern half of the tribe of Manasseh settled on the eastern side of the Jordan River, they built a monument to show they belonged to God (Jos 22:9–12). The monument was so large that the tribes west of the Jordan mistook it as a sign of aggression (v.13–29). When the western tribes confronted the eastern tribes, they learned the altar was not a symbol of division, but of solidarity with their countrymen in Canaan (v.30–31). The monument served as a declaration and a reminder that the Lord is God (v.34).

Joshua gathered God's people for a covenant renewal ceremony to remind them who they were and whom they served (Jos 24:14–28). This was done to remind the people of the covenant the Lord swore to their forefather Abraham (Gen 12:2). Joshua recounted how the Lord had delivered them against impossible odds to this place and called for them to cleanse themselves from idolatry to worship the Lord alone (Jos 24:14–15). To commemorate the moment, Joshua set up a stone at Shechem, which stood as a witness to the day and place where God's people recommitted to His covenant and provision.

"I will not leave you or abandon you."

JOSHUA 1:5

God Encourages Joshua

Throughout the book of Joshua, we'll encounter many moments where the people of God stopped to remember God and His covenant with them. Each of these moments is discussed in more detail on pages 18–21 and will be marked with a symbol in the margins.

Joshua 1
ENCOURAGEMENT OF JOSHUA

¹ After the death of Moses the Lord's servant, the Lord spoke to Joshua son of Nun, Moses's assistant: ² "Moses my servant is dead. Now you and all the people prepare to cross over the Jordan to the land I am giving the Israelites. ³ I have given you every place where the sole of your foot treads, just as I promised Moses. ⁴ Your territory will be from the wilderness and Lebanon to the great river, the Euphrates River—all the land of the Hittites—and west to the Mediterranean Sea. ⁵ No one will be able to stand against you as long as you live. I will be with you, just as I was with Moses. I will not leave you or abandon you.

⁶ "Be strong and courageous, for you will distribute the land I swore to their ancestors to give them as an inheritance. ⁷ Above all, be strong and very courageous to observe carefully the whole instruction my servant Moses commanded you. Do not turn from it to the right or the left,

so that you will have success wherever you go. [8] This book of instruction must not depart from your mouth; you are to meditate on it day and night so that you may carefully observe everything written in it. For then you will prosper and succeed in whatever you do. [9] Haven't I commanded you: be strong and courageous? Do not be afraid or discouraged, for the LORD your God is with you wherever you go."

JOSHUA PREPARES THE PEOPLE

[10] Then Joshua commanded the officers of the people, [11] "Go through the camp and tell the people, 'Get provisions ready for yourselves, for within three days you will be crossing the Jordan to go in and take possession of the land the LORD your God is giving you to inherit.'"

[12] Joshua said to the Reubenites, the Gadites, and half the tribe of Manasseh, [13] "Remember what Moses the LORD's servant commanded you when he said,

'The LORD your God will give you rest, and he will give you this land.'

[14] Your wives, dependents, and livestock may remain in the land Moses gave you on this side of the Jordan. But your best soldiers must cross over in battle formation ahead of your brothers and help them [15] until the LORD gives your brothers rest, as he has given you, and they too possess the land the LORD your God is giving them. You may then return to the land of your inheritance and take possession of what Moses the LORD's servant gave you on the east side of the Jordan."

[16] They answered Joshua, "Everything you have commanded us we will do, and everywhere you send us we will go. [17] We will obey you, just as we obeyed Moses in everything. Certainly the LORD your God will be with you, as he was with Moses. [18] Anyone who rebels against your order and does not obey your words in all that you command him, will be put to death. Above all, be strong and courageous!"

Genesis 15:18–21

[18] On that day the LORD made a covenant with Abram, saying, "I give this land to your offspring, from the Brook of Egypt to the great river, the Euphrates River: [19] the land of the Kenites, Kenizzites, Kadmonites, [20] Hethites, Perizzites, Rephaim, [21] Amorites, Canaanites, Girgashites, and Jebusites."

Deuteronomy 31:1–6
JOSHUA TAKES MOSES'S PLACE

[1] Then Moses continued to speak these words to all Israel, [2] saying, "I am now 120 years old; I can no longer act as your leader. The LORD has told me, 'You will not cross the Jordan.' [3] The LORD your God is the one who will cross ahead of you. He will destroy these nations before you, and you will drive them out. Joshua is the one who will cross ahead of you, as the LORD has said. [4] The LORD will deal with them as he did Sihon and Og, the kings of the Amorites, and their land when he destroyed them. [5] The LORD will deliver them over to you, and you must do to them exactly as I have commanded you. [6] Be strong and courageous; don't be terrified or afraid of them. For the LORD your God is the one who will go with you; he will not leave you or abandon you."

1 Thessalonians 5:23–24

[23] Now may the God of peace himself sanctify you completely. And may your whole spirit, soul, and body be kept sound and blameless at the coming of our Lord Jesus Christ. [24] He who calls you is faithful; he will do it.

DATE

Rahab & the Spies

Joshua 2
SPIES SENT TO JERICHO

¹ Joshua son of Nun secretly sent two men as spies from the Acacia Grove, saying, "Go and scout the land, especially Jericho." So they left, and they came to the house of a prostitute named Rahab, and stayed there.

² The king of Jericho was told, "Look, some of the Israelite men have come here tonight to investigate the land." ³ Then the king of Jericho sent word to Rahab and said, "Bring out the men who came to you and entered your house, for they came to investigate the entire land."

⁴ But the woman had taken the two men and hidden them. So she said, "Yes, the men did come to me, but I didn't know where they were from. ⁵ At nightfall, when the city gate was about to close, the men went out, and I don't know where they were going. Chase after them quickly, and you can catch up with them!" ⁶ But she had taken them up to the roof and hidden them among the stalks of flax that she had arranged on the roof. ⁷ The men pursued them along the road to the fords of the Jordan, and as soon as they left to pursue them, the city gate was shut.

⁸ Before the men fell asleep, she went up on the roof ⁹ and said to them, "I know that the LORD has given you this land and that the terror of you has fallen on us, and everyone who lives in the land is panicking because of you. ¹⁰ For we have heard how the LORD dried up the water of the Red Sea before you when you came out of Egypt, and what you did to Sihon and Og, the two Amorite kings you completely destroyed across the Jordan. ¹¹ When we heard this, we lost heart, and everyone's courage failed because of you, for the LORD your God is God in heaven above and on earth below. ¹² Now please swear to me by the LORD that you will also show kindness to my father's family, because I showed kindness to you. Give me a sure sign ¹³ that you will spare the lives of my father, mother, brothers, sisters, and all who belong to them, and save us from death."

¹⁴ The men answered her, "We will give our lives for yours. If you don't report our mission, we will show kindness and faithfulness to you when the LORD gives us the land."

¹⁵ Then she let them down by a rope through the window, since she lived in a house that was built into the wall of the city. ¹⁶ "Go to the hill country so that the men pursuing you won't find you," she said to them. "Hide there for three days until they return; afterward, go on your way."

¹⁷ The men said to her, "We will be free from this oath you made us swear, ¹⁸ unless, when we enter the land, you tie this scarlet cord to the window through which you let us down. Bring your father, mother, brothers, and all your father's family into your house. ¹⁹ If anyone goes out the doors of your house, his death will be his own fault, and we will be innocent. But if anyone with you in the house should be harmed, his death will be our fault. ²⁰ And if you report our mission, we are free from the oath you made us swear."

²¹ "Let it be as you say," she replied, and she sent them away. After they had gone, she tied the scarlet cord to the window.

²² So the two men went into the hill country and stayed there three days until the pursuers had returned. They searched all along the way, but did not find them. ²³ Then the men returned, came down from the hill country, and crossed the Jordan. They went to Joshua son of Nun and reported everything that had happened to them. ²⁴ They told Joshua, "The LORD has handed over the entire land to us. Everyone who lives in the land is also panicking because of us."

Numbers 13:26–33
REPORT ABOUT CANAAN

²⁶ The men went back to Moses, Aaron, and the entire Israelite community in the Wilderness of Paran at Kadesh. They brought back a report for them and the whole community, and they showed them the fruit of the land. ²⁷ They reported to Moses, "We went into the land where you sent us. Indeed it is flowing with milk and honey, and here is some of its fruit. ²⁸ However, the people living in the land are strong, and the cities are large and fortified. We also saw the descendants of Anak there. ²⁹ The Amalekites are living in the land of the Negev; the Hethites, Jebusites, and Amorites live in the hill country; and the Canaanites live by the sea and along the Jordan."

³⁰ Then Caleb quieted the people in the presence of Moses and said, "Let's go up now and take possession of the land because we can certainly conquer it!"

³¹ But the men who had gone up with him responded, "We can't attack the people because they are stronger than we are!" ³² So they gave a negative report to the Israelites about the land they had scouted: "The land we passed through to explore is one that devours its inhabitants, and all the people we saw in it are men of great size. ³³ We even saw the Nephilim there—the descendants of Anak come from the Nephilim! To ourselves we seemed like grasshoppers, and we must have seemed the same to them."

Hebrews 11:31

By faith Rahab the prostitute welcomed the spies in peace and didn't perish with those who disobeyed.

DATE

Consecrate yourselves, because the LORD will do wonders among you tomorrow.

JOSHUA 3:5

Crossing the Jordan

Joshua 3
CROSSING THE JORDAN

¹ Joshua started early the next morning and left the Acacia Grove with all the Israelites. They went as far as the Jordan and stayed there before crossing. ² After three days the officers went through the camp ³ and commanded the people, "When you see the ark of the covenant of the LORD your God carried by the Levitical priests, you are to break camp and follow it. ⁴ But keep a distance of about a thousand yards between yourselves and the ark. Don't go near it, so that you can see the way to go, for you haven't traveled this way before."

⁵ Joshua told the people, "Consecrate yourselves, because the LORD will do wonders among you tomorrow." ⁶ Then he said to the priests, "Carry the ark of the covenant and go on ahead of the people." So they carried the ark of the covenant and went ahead of them.

⁷ The LORD spoke to Joshua: "Today I will begin to exalt you in the sight of all Israel, so they will know that I will be with you just as I was with Moses. ⁸ Command the priests carrying the ark of the covenant: When you reach the edge of the water, stand in the Jordan."

9 Then Joshua told the Israelites, "Come closer and listen to the words of the LORD your God." 10 He said, "You will know that the living God is among you and that he will certainly dispossess before you the Canaanites, Hethites, Hivites, Perizzites, Girgashites, Amorites, and Jebusites 11 when the ark of the covenant of the Lord of the whole earth goes ahead of you into the Jordan. 12 Now choose twelve men from the tribes of Israel, one man for each tribe. 13 When the feet of the priests who carry the ark of the LORD, the Lord of the whole earth, come to rest in the Jordan's water, its water will be cut off. The water flowing downstream will stand up in a mass."

14 When the people broke camp to cross the Jordan, the priests carried the ark of the covenant ahead of the people. 15 Now the Jordan overflows its banks throughout the harvest season. But as soon as the priests carrying the ark reached the Jordan, their feet touched the water at its edge 16 and the water flowing downstream stood still, rising up in a mass that extended as far as Adam, a city next to Zarethan. The water flowing downstream into the Sea of the Arabah—the Dead Sea—was completely cut off, and the people crossed opposite Jericho. 17 The priests carrying the ark of the LORD's covenant stood firmly on dry ground in the middle of the Jordan, while all Israel crossed on dry ground until the entire nation had finished crossing the Jordan.

Exodus 25:10–22
THE ARK

10 "They are to make an ark of acacia wood, forty-five inches long, twenty-seven inches wide, and twenty-seven inches high. 11 Overlay it with pure gold; overlay it both inside and out. Also make a gold molding all around it. 12 Cast four gold rings for it and place them on its four feet, two rings on one side and two rings on the other side. 13 Make poles of acacia wood and overlay them with gold. 14 Insert the poles into the rings on the sides of the ark in order to carry the ark with them. 15 The poles are to remain in the rings of the ark; they must not be removed from it. 16 Put the tablets of the testimony that I will give you into the ark. 17 Make a mercy seat of pure gold, forty-five inches long and twenty-seven inches wide. 18 Make two cherubim of gold; make them of hammered work at the two ends of the mercy seat. 19 Make

one cherub at one end and one cherub at the other end. At its two ends, make the cherubim of one piece with the mercy seat. 20 The cherubim are to have wings spread out above, covering the mercy seat with their wings, and are to face one another. The faces of the cherubim should be toward the mercy seat. 21 Set the mercy seat on top of the ark and put the tablets of the testimony that I will give you into the ark.

22 I will meet with you there above the mercy seat, between the two cherubim that are over the ark of the testimony;

I will speak with you from there about all that I command you regarding the Israelites."

Hebrews 10:19–22

19 Therefore, brothers and sisters, since we have boldness to enter the sanctuary through the blood of Jesus— 20 he has inaugurated for us a new and living way through the curtain (that is, through his flesh)— 21 and since we have a great high priest over the house of God, 22 let us draw near with a true heart in full assurance of faith, with our hearts sprinkled clean from an evil conscience and our bodies washed in pure water.

DATE

On Jordan's Stormy Banks

WORDS
Samuel Stennett

MUSIC
American Folk Hymn;
arr. Rigdon M. McIntosh

On Jordan's stormy banks I stand
and cast a wishful eye
to Canaan's fair and happy land,
Where my possessions lie.

Chorus:
I am bound for the promised land,
I am bound for the promised land;
O who will come and go with me?
I am bound for the promised land.

All o'er those wide extended plains
shines one eternal day;
There God the Son forever reigns
and scatters night away.

Chorus

No chilling winds nor pois'nous breath
can reach that healthful shore;
Sickness and sorrow, pain and death
are felt and feared no more.

Chorus

When shall I reach that happy place
and be forever blest?
When shall I see my Father's face
and in His bosom rest?

Chorus

1. On Jor-dan's storm-y banks I stand and cast a wish-ful eye
2. All o'er those wide-ex-tend-ed plains shines one e-ter-nal day;
3. No chill-ing winds nor pois-'nous breath can reach that health-ful shore;
4. When shall I reach that hap-py place and be for-ev-er blest?

to Ca-naan's fair and hap-py land, Where my pos-ses-sions lie.
There God the Son for-ev-er reigns and scat-ters night a-way.
Sick-ness and sor-row, pain and death are felt and feared no more.
When shall I see my Fa-ther's face and in His bos-om rest?

Chorus

I am bound for the prom-ised land, I am bound for the prom-ised land;

O who will come and go with me? I am bound for the prom-ised land.

Memorial Stones

Joshua 4

THE MEMORIAL STONES

¹ After the entire nation had finished crossing the Jordan, the LORD spoke to Joshua: ² "Choose twelve men from the people, one man for each tribe, ³ and command them: Take twelve stones from this place in the middle of the Jordan where the priests are standing, carry them with you, and set them down at the place where you spend the night."

⁴ So Joshua summoned the twelve men he had selected from the Israelites, one man for each tribe, ⁵ and said to them, "Go across to the ark of the LORD your God in the middle of the Jordan. Each of you lift a stone onto his shoulder, one for each of the Israelite tribes, ⁶ so that this will be a sign among you. In the future, when your children ask you, 'What do these stones mean to you?' ⁷ you should tell them, 'The water of the Jordan was cut off in front of the ark of the LORD's covenant. When it crossed the Jordan, the Jordan's water was cut off.' Therefore these stones will always be a memorial for the Israelites."

⁸ The Israelites did just as Joshua had commanded them. The twelve men took stones from the middle of the Jordan, one for each of the Israelite tribes, just as the LORD had told Joshua. They carried them to the camp and set them down there. ⁹ Joshua also set up twelve stones in the middle of the Jordan where the priests who carried the ark of the covenant were standing. The stones are still there today.

¹⁰ The priests carrying the ark continued standing in the middle of the Jordan until everything was completed that the LORD had commanded Joshua to tell the people, in keeping with all that Moses had commanded Joshua. The people hurried across, ¹¹ and after everyone had finished crossing, the priests with the ark of the LORD crossed in the sight of the people. ¹² The Reubenites, Gadites, and half the tribe of Manasseh went in battle formation in front of the Israelites, as Moses had instructed them. ¹³ About forty thousand equipped for war crossed to the plains of Jericho in the LORD's presence.

¹⁴ On that day the LORD exalted Joshua in the sight of all Israel, and they revered him throughout his life, as they had revered Moses. ¹⁵ The LORD told Joshua, ¹⁶ "Command the priests who carry the ark of the testimony to come up from the Jordan."

¹⁷ So Joshua commanded the priests, "Come up from the Jordan." ¹⁸ When the priests carrying the ark of the LORD's covenant came up from the middle of the Jordan, and their feet stepped out on solid ground, the water of the Jordan resumed its course, flowing over all the banks as before.

¹⁹ The people came up from the Jordan on the tenth day of the first month, and camped at Gilgal on the eastern limits of Jericho. ²⁰ Then Joshua set up in Gilgal the twelve stones they had taken from the Jordan, ²¹ and he said to the Israelites, "In the future, when your children ask their fathers, 'What is the meaning of these stones?' ²² you should tell your children, 'Israel crossed the Jordan on dry ground.' ²³ For the LORD your God dried up the water of the Jordan before you until you had crossed over, just as the LORD your God did to the Red Sea, which he dried up before us until we had crossed over. ²⁴ This is so that all the peoples of the earth may know that the LORD's hand is strong, and so that you may always fear the LORD your God."

Joshua 5:1–9
CIRCUMCISION OF THE ISRAELITES

¹ When all the Amorite kings across the Jordan to the west and all the Canaanite kings near the sea heard how the LORD had dried up the water of the Jordan before the Israelites until they had crossed over, they lost heart and their courage failed because of the Israelites.

² At that time the LORD said to Joshua, "Make flint knives and circumcise the Israelite men again." ³ So Joshua made flint knives and circumcised the Israelite men at Gibeath-haaraloth. ⁴ This is the reason Joshua circumcised them: All the people who came out of Egypt who were males—all the men of war—had died in the wilderness along the way after they had come out of Egypt. ⁵ Though all the people who came out were circumcised, none of the people born in the wilderness along the way were circumcised after they

had come out of Egypt. ⁶ For the Israelites wandered in the wilderness forty years until all the nation's men of war who came out of Egypt had died off because they did not obey the LORD. So the LORD vowed never to let them see the land he had sworn to their ancestors to give us, a land flowing with milk and honey. ⁷ He raised up their sons in their place; it was these Joshua circumcised. They were still uncircumcised, since they had not been circumcised along the way. ⁸ After the entire nation had been circumcised, they stayed where they were in the camp until they recovered. ⁹ The LORD then said to Joshua, "Today I have rolled away the disgrace of Egypt from you." Therefore, that place is still called Gilgal today.

Exodus 14:21–25, 30–31
²¹ Then Moses stretched out his hand over the sea. The LORD drove the sea back with a powerful east wind all that night and turned the sea into dry land. So the waters were divided, ²² and the Israelites went through the sea on dry ground, with the waters like a wall to them on their right and their left.

²³ The Egyptians set out in pursuit—all Pharaoh's horses, his chariots, and his horsemen—and went into the sea after them. ²⁴ During the morning watch, the LORD looked down at the Egyptian forces from the pillar of fire and cloud, and threw the Egyptian forces into confusion. ²⁵ He caused their chariot wheels to swerve and made them drive with difficulty. "Let's get away from Israel," the Egyptians said, "because the LORD is fighting for them against Egypt!"

…

³⁰ That day the LORD saved Israel from the power of the Egyptians, and Israel saw the Egyptians dead on the seashore. ³¹ When Israel saw the great power that the LORD used against the Egyptians, the people feared the LORD and believed in him and in his servant Moses.

Colossians 2:11–12
¹¹ You were also circumcised in him with a circumcision not done with hands, by putting off the body of flesh, in the circumcision of Christ, ¹² when you were buried with him in baptism, in which you were also raised with him through faith in the working of God, who raised him from the dead.

DATE

The Conquest of Jericho

DAY 5

Joshua 5:10–15
Joshua 6
Exodus 3:1–6
Romans 8:31

EIN GEDI • JUDAH

(4) Joshua 5:10–15

FOOD FROM THE LAND

¹⁰ While the Israelites camped at Gilgal on the plains of Jericho, they observed the Passover on the evening of the fourteenth day of the month. ¹¹ The day after Passover they ate unleavened bread and roasted grain from the produce of the land. ¹² And the day after they ate from the produce of the land, the manna ceased. Since there was no more manna for the Israelites, they ate from the crops of the land of Canaan that year.

COMMANDER OF THE LORD'S ARMY

¹³ When Joshua was near Jericho, he looked up and saw a man standing in front of him with a drawn sword in his hand. Joshua approached him and asked, "Are you for us or for our enemies?"

¹⁴ "Neither," he replied. "I have now come as commander of the LORD's army."

Then Joshua bowed with his face to the ground in homage and asked him, "What does my lord want to say to his servant?"

¹⁵ The commander of the LORD's army said to Joshua, "Remove the sandals from your feet, for the place where you are standing is holy." And Joshua did that.

Joshua 6

THE CONQUEST OF JERICHO

¹ Now Jericho was strongly fortified because of the Israelites—no one leaving or entering. ² The LORD said to Joshua, "Look, I have handed Jericho, its king, and its best soldiers over to you. ³ March around the city with all the men of war, circling the city one time. Do this for six days. ⁴ Have seven priests carry seven ram's-horn trumpets in front of the ark. But on the seventh day, march around the city seven times, while the priests blow the ram's horns. ⁵ When there is a prolonged blast of the horn and you hear its sound, have all the troops give a mighty shout. Then the city wall will collapse, and the troops will advance, each man straight ahead."

⁶ So Joshua son of Nun summoned the priests and said to them, "Take up the ark of the covenant and have seven priests carry seven ram's horns in front of the ark of the LORD." ⁷ He said to the troops, "Move forward, march around the city, and have the armed men go ahead of the ark of the LORD."

⁸ After Joshua had spoken to the troops, seven priests carrying seven ram's horns before the LORD moved forward and blew the ram's horns; the ark of the LORD's covenant followed them. ⁹ While the ram's horns were blowing, the armed men went in front of the priests who blew the ram's horns, and the rear guard went behind the ark. ¹⁰ But Joshua had commanded the troops, "Do not shout or let your voice be heard. Don't let one word come out of your mouth until the time I say, 'Shout!' Then you are to shout." ¹¹ So the ark of the LORD was carried around the city, circling it once. They returned to the camp and spent the night there.

¹² Joshua got up early the next morning. The priests took the ark of the LORD, ¹³ and the seven priests carrying seven ram's horns marched in front of the ark of the LORD. While the ram's horns were blowing, the armed men went in front of them, and the rear guard went behind the ark of the LORD. ¹⁴ On the second day they marched around the city once and returned to the camp. They did this for six days.

¹⁵ Early on the seventh day, they started at dawn and marched around the city seven times in the same way. That was the only day they marched around the city seven times. ¹⁶ After the seventh time, the priests blew the ram's horns, and Joshua said to the troops, "Shout! For the LORD has given you the city. ¹⁷ But the city and everything in it are set apart to the LORD for destruction. Only Rahab the prostitute and everyone with her in the house will live, because she hid the messengers we sent. ¹⁸ But keep yourselves from the things set apart, or you will be set apart for destruction. If you take any of those things, you will set apart the camp of Israel for destruction and make trouble for it. ¹⁹ For all the silver and gold, and the articles of bronze and iron, are dedicated to the LORD and must go into the LORD's treasury."

²⁰ So the troops shouted, and the ram's horns sounded. When they heard the blast of the ram's horn, the troops gave a great shout, and the wall collapsed. The troops advanced into the

city, each man straight ahead, and they captured the city. [21] They completely destroyed everything in the city with the sword—every man and woman, both young and old, and every ox, sheep, and donkey.

RAHAB AND HER FAMILY SPARED

[22] Joshua said to the two men who had scouted the land, "Go to the prostitute's house and bring the woman out of there, and all who are with her, just as you swore to her." [23] So the young men who had scouted went in and brought out Rahab and her father, mother, brothers, and all who belonged to her. They brought out her whole family and settled them outside the camp of Israel.

[24] They burned the city and everything in it, but they put the silver and gold and the articles of bronze and iron into the treasury of the LORD's house.

[25] However, Joshua spared Rahab the prostitute, her father's family, and all who belonged to her,

because she hid the messengers Joshua had sent to spy on Jericho, and she still lives in Israel today.

[26] At that time Joshua imposed this curse:

The man who undertakes
the rebuilding of this city, Jericho,
is cursed before the LORD.
He will lay its foundation
at the cost of his firstborn;
he will finish its gates
at the cost of his youngest.

[27] And the LORD was with Joshua, and his fame spread throughout the land.

Exodus 3:1–6
MOSES AND THE BURNING BUSH

[1] Meanwhile, Moses was shepherding the flock of his father-in-law Jethro, the priest of Midian. He led the flock to the far side of the wilderness and came to Horeb, the mountain of God. [2] Then the angel of the LORD appeared to him in a flame of fire within a bush. As Moses looked, he saw that the bush was on fire but was not consumed. [3] So Moses thought, "I must go over and look at this remarkable sight. Why isn't the bush burning up?"

[4] When the LORD saw that he had gone over to look, God called out to him from the bush, "Moses, Moses!"

"Here I am," he answered.

[5] "Do not come closer," he said. "Remove the sandals from your feet, for the place where you are standing is holy ground." [6] Then he continued, "I am the God of your father, the God of Abraham, the God of Isaac, and the God of Jacob." Moses hid his face because he was afraid to look at God.

Romans 8:31

What, then, are we to say about these things? If God is for us, who is against us?

DATE

REFLECT & REMEMBER

In Joshua, stones or stone altars were often used to mark places where God's presence was evident or to memorialize fulfilled promises. Joshua 4 includes a detailed account of how the use of memorial stones helped God's people remember His faithfulness. We, too, are called to remember and proclaim God's work in our lives (2Pt 1:12).

"I am with you always."

MATTHEW 28:20

Use this journaling space to reflect on a time when you felt God's presence with you during an activity, conversation, or something else He called you to. Let this written account be your personal stone of remembrance to mark God's work in your life for you to look back on in the days to come.

DAY 6: GRACE DAY

*Take this day to catch up on
your reading, pray, and rest
in the presence of the Lord.*

He who calls you is faithful; he will do it.

1 THESSALONIANS 5:24

WEEKLY

DAY 7

Scripture is God-breathed and true. When we memorize it, we carry His Word with us wherever we go.

During this reading plan, we will memorize Joshua 1:9. This week, focus on memorizing just the first part. Try saying it aloud three times, writing it down three times, and repeating the pattern to help you remember.

"Haven't I commanded you: be strong and courageous?

Do not be afraid or discouraged,

for the LORD your God is with you wherever you go."

JOSHUA 1:9

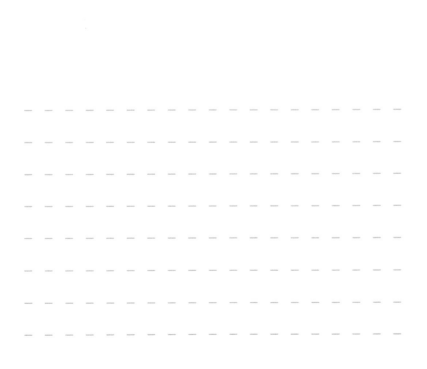

Achan's Disobedience

Joshua 7

DEFEAT AT AI

[1] The Israelites, however, were unfaithful regarding the things set apart for destruction. Achan son of Carmi, son of Zabdi, son of Zerah, of the tribe of Judah, took some of what was set apart, and the LORD's anger burned against the Israelites.

[2] Joshua sent men from Jericho to Ai, which is near Beth-aven, east of Bethel, and told them, "Go up and scout the land." So the men went up and scouted Ai.

[3] After returning to Joshua they reported to him, "Don't send all the people, but send about two thousand or three thousand men to attack Ai. Since the people of Ai are so few, don't wear out all our people there." [4] So about three thousand men went up there, but they fled from the men of Ai. [5] The men of Ai struck down about thirty-six of them and chased them from outside the city gate to the quarries, striking them down on the descent. As a result, the people lost heart.

6 Then Joshua tore his clothes and fell facedown to the ground before the ark of the LORD until evening, as did the elders of Israel; they all put dust on their heads. 7 "Oh, Lord GOD," Joshua said, "why did you ever bring these people across the Jordan to hand us over to the Amorites for our destruction? If only we had been content to remain on the other side of the Jordan! 8 What can I say, Lord, now that Israel has turned its back and run from its enemies? 9 When the Canaanites and all who live in the land hear about this, they will surround us and wipe out our name from the earth. Then what will you do about your great name?"

10 The LORD then said to Joshua, "Stand up! Why have you fallen facedown? 11 Israel has sinned. They have violated my covenant that I appointed for them. They have taken some of what was set apart. They have stolen, deceived, and put those things with their own belongings. 12 This is why the Israelites cannot stand against their enemies. They will turn their backs and run from their enemies, because they have been set apart for destruction. I will no longer be with you unless you remove from among you what is set apart.

13 "Go and consecrate the people.

Tell them to consecrate themselves for tomorrow, for this is what the LORD, the God of Israel, says: There are things that are set apart among you, Israel. You will not be able to stand against your enemies until you remove what is set apart. 14 In the morning, present yourselves tribe by tribe. The tribe the LORD selects is to come forward clan by clan. The clan the LORD selects is to come forward family by family. The family the LORD selects is to come forward man by man. 15 The one who is caught with the things set apart must be burned, along with everything he has, because he has violated the LORD's covenant and committed an outrage in Israel."

ACHAN JUDGED

16 Joshua got up early the next morning. He had Israel come forward tribe by tribe, and the tribe of Judah was selected. 17 He had the clans of Judah come forward, and the Zerahite clan was selected. He had the Zerahite clan come forward by heads of families, and Zabdi was selected. 18 He then had Zabdi's family come forward man by man, and Achan son of Carmi, son of Zabdi, son of Zerah, of the tribe of Judah, was selected.

19 So Joshua said to Achan, "My son, give glory to the LORD, the God of Israel, and make a confession to him. I urge you, tell me what you have done. Don't hide anything from me."

20 Achan replied to Joshua, "It is true. I have sinned against the LORD, the God of Israel. This is what I did: 21 When I saw among the spoils a beautiful cloak from Babylon, five pounds of silver, and a bar of gold weighing a pound and a quarter, I coveted them and took them. You can see for yourself. They are concealed in the ground inside my tent, with the silver under the cloak." 22 So Joshua sent messengers who ran to the tent, and there was the cloak, concealed in his tent, with the silver underneath. 23 They took the things from inside the tent, brought them to Joshua and all the Israelites, and spread them out in the LORD's presence.

24 Then Joshua and all Israel with him took Achan son of Zerah, the silver, the cloak, and the bar of gold, his sons and daughters, his ox, donkey, and sheep, his tent, and all that he had, and brought them up to the Valley of Achor. 25 Joshua said, "Why have you brought us trouble? Today the LORD will bring you trouble!" So all Israel stoned them to death. They burned their bodies, threw stones on them, 26 and raised over him a large pile of rocks that remains still today. Then the LORD turned from his burning anger. Therefore that place is called the Valley of Achor still today.

Deuteronomy 9:26–29
26 I prayed to the LORD:

Lord GOD, do not annihilate your people, your inheritance, whom you redeemed through your greatness and brought out of Egypt with a strong hand. 27 Remember your servants Abraham, Isaac, and Jacob. Disregard this people's stubbornness, and their wickedness and sin. 28 Otherwise, those in the land you brought us from will say, "Because the LORD wasn't able to bring them into the land he had promised them, and because he hated them, he brought them out to kill them in the wilderness." [29] But they are your people, your inheritance, whom you brought out by your great power and outstretched arm.

Hosea 2:15

"There I will give her vineyards back to her
and make the Valley of Achor
into a gateway of hope.
There she will respond as she did
in the days of her youth,
as in the day she came out of the land of Egypt."

James 1:19–25
HEARING AND DOING THE WORD

[19] My dear brothers and sisters, understand this: Everyone should be quick to listen, slow to speak, and slow to anger, [20] for human anger does not accomplish God's righteousness. [21] Therefore, ridding yourselves of all moral filth and the evil that is so prevalent, humbly receive the implanted word, which is able to save your souls.

[22] But be doers of the word and not hearers only, deceiving yourselves. [23] Because if anyone is a hearer of the word and not a doer, he is like someone looking at his own face in a mirror. [24] For he looks at himself, goes away, and immediately forgets what kind of person he was. [25] But the one who looks intently into the perfect law of freedom and perseveres in it, and is not a forgetful hearer but a doer who works—this person will be blessed in what he does.

DATE

The True People of God

*And if you belong to Christ, then you are Abraham's seed,
heirs according to the promise.*

GALATIANS 3:29

———————————

In the time of the Old Testament, Israel was set apart as the people of God. As Abraham's descendants, the nation enjoyed unique access to God's mercy, provision, presence, and protection. But what does it mean to truly be the people of God?

The New Testament tells us that all who follow Jesus are the true people of God and children of Abraham by faith. Regardless of earthly bloodline, all people have access to be counted as God's people through faith. The stories of Achan and Rahab in the book of Joshua are two examples in the Old Testament of this broader narrative of God's family in Scripture. Here is a comparison between Achan, an Israelite by birth, and Rahab, who was brought into the family of God through faith.

ACHAN	**RAHAB**
Israelite, from the tribe of Judah. JOS 7:1	Prostitute, from the pagan city of Jericho. JOS 2:1
As an Israelite, had access to God but did not fear Him. JOS 7:10-11	As a Canaanite, did not have access to God but feared Him. JOS 2:8-13
Directly disobeyed God by preserving the spoils of Jericho for himself; hid them in his tent. JOS 7:21	Directly disobeyed the king of Jericho to preserve the lives of the two spies; hid them on her rooftop. JOS 2:3-6
Confessed sinning against God. JOS 7:19-20	Confessed belief in the God of the Israelites. JOS 2:9-11
Brought judgment and destruction on his family and Israel through disobedience and greed. JOS 7:12, 24-25	Brought salvation and deliverance to her family through faith. JOS 6:25
Cut off from Israel, even though he was a citizen by birth. Had no descendants. JOS 7:24-25	Joined Israel, even though she was a Canaanite by birth. Direct ancestor to King David and included in the genealogy of Jesus. JOS 6:25; MT 1:5
Remembered for his disobedience. JOS 7:25-26	Remembered for her faith. HEB 11:31

Conquest & Commitment

DAY 9

Joshua 8
Exodus 20:22–24
Hebrews 8:8–12

NAZARETH · ZEBULUN

Joshua 8
CONQUEST OF AI

¹ The LORD said to Joshua, "Do not be afraid or discouraged. Take all the troops with you and go attack Ai. Look, I have handed over to you the king of Ai, his people, city, and land. ² Treat Ai and its king as you did Jericho and its king, except that you may plunder its spoil and livestock for yourselves. Set an ambush behind the city."

³ So Joshua and all the troops set out to attack Ai. Joshua selected thirty thousand of his best soldiers and sent them out at night. ⁴ He commanded them, "Pay attention. Lie in ambush behind the city, not too far from it, and all of you be ready. ⁵ Then I and all the people who are with me will approach the city. When they come out against us as they did the first time, we will flee from them. ⁶ They will come after us until we have drawn them away from the city, for they will say, 'They are fleeing from us as before.' While we are fleeing from them, ⁷ you are to come out of your ambush and seize the city. The LORD your God will hand it over to you. ⁸ After taking the city, set it on fire. Follow the LORD's command— see that you do as I have ordered you." ⁹ So Joshua sent them out, and they went to the ambush site and waited between Bethel and Ai, to the west of Ai. But he spent that night with the troops.

¹⁰ Joshua started early the next morning and mobilized them. Then he and the elders of Israel led the people up to Ai. ¹¹ All the troops who were with him went up and approached the city, arriving opposite Ai, and camped to the north of it, with a valley between them and the city. ¹² Now Joshua had taken about five thousand men and set them in ambush between Bethel and Ai, to the west of the city. ¹³ The troops were stationed in this way: the main camp to the north of the city and its rear guard to the west of the city. And that night Joshua went into the valley.

¹⁴ When the king of Ai saw the Israelites, the men of the city hurried and went out early in the morning so that he and all his people could engage Israel in battle at a suitable place facing the Arabah. But he did not know there was an ambush waiting for him behind the city. ¹⁵ Joshua and all Israel pretended to be beaten back by them and fled toward the wilderness. ¹⁶ Then all the troops of Ai were summoned

to pursue them, and they pursued Joshua and were drawn away from the city. ¹⁷ Not a man was left in Ai or Bethel who did not go out after Israel, leaving the city exposed while they pursued Israel.

¹⁸ Then the LORD said to Joshua, "Hold out the javelin in your hand toward Ai, for I will hand the city over to you." So Joshua held out his javelin toward it. ¹⁹ When he held out his hand, the men in ambush rose quickly from their position. They ran, entered the city, captured it, and immediately set it on fire.

²⁰ The men of Ai turned and looked back, and smoke from the city was rising to the sky! They could not escape in any direction, and the troops who had fled to the wilderness now became the pursuers. ²¹ When Joshua and all Israel saw that the men in ambush had captured the city and that smoke was rising from it, they turned back and struck down the men of Ai. ²² Then men in ambush came out of the city against them, and the men of Ai were trapped between the Israelite forces, some on one side and some on the other. They struck them down until no survivor or fugitive remained, ²³ but they captured the king of Ai alive and brought him to Joshua.

²⁴ When Israel had finished killing everyone living in Ai who had pursued them into the open country, and when every last one of them had fallen by the sword, all Israel returned to Ai and struck it down with the sword. ²⁵ The total of those who fell that day, both men and women, was twelve thousand—all the people of Ai. ²⁶ Joshua did not draw back his hand that was holding the javelin until all the inhabitants of Ai were completely destroyed. ²⁷ Israel plundered only the cattle and spoil of that city for themselves, according to the LORD's command that he had given Joshua.

²⁸ Joshua burned Ai and left it a permanent ruin, still desolate today. ²⁹ He hung the body of the king of Ai on a tree until evening, and at sunset Joshua commanded that they take his body down from the tree. They threw it down at the entrance of the city gate and put a large pile of rocks over it, which still remains today.

RENEWED COMMITMENT TO THE LAW

⁵

³⁰ At that time Joshua built an altar on Mount Ebal to the Lord, the God of Israel, ³¹ just as Moses the Lord's servant had commanded the Israelites. He built it according to what is written in the book of the law of Moses: an altar of uncut stones on which no iron tool has been used. Then they offered burnt offerings to the Lord and sacrificed fellowship offerings on it. ³² There on the stones, Joshua copied the law of Moses, which he had written in the presence of the Israelites. ³³ All Israel—resident alien and citizen alike—with their elders, officers, and judges, stood on either side of the ark of the Lord's covenant facing the Levitical priests who carried it. Half of them were in front of Mount Gerizim and half in front of Mount Ebal, as Moses the Lord's servant had commanded earlier concerning blessing the people of Israel. ³⁴ Afterward, Joshua read aloud all the words of the law—the blessings as well as the curses—according to all that is written in the book of the law. ³⁵ There was not a word of all that Moses had commanded that Joshua did not read before the entire assembly of Israel, including the women, the dependents, and the resident aliens who lived among them.

Exodus 20:22–24
MOSES RECEIVES ADDITIONAL LAWS

²² Then the Lord told Moses, "This is what you are to say to the Israelites: You have seen that I have spoken to you from heaven. ²³ Do not make gods of silver to rival me; do not make gods of gold for yourselves.

²⁴ "Make an earthen altar for me, and sacrifice on it your burnt offerings and fellowship offerings, your flocks and herds.

I will come to you and bless you in every place where I cause my name to be remembered."

Hebrews 8:8–12
⁸ But finding fault with his people, he says:

See, the days are coming, says the Lord,
when I will make a new covenant
with the house of Israel
and with the house of Judah—
⁹ not like the covenant
that I made with their ancestors
on the day I took them by the hand
to lead them out of the land of Egypt.
I showed no concern for them, says the Lord,
because they did not continue in my covenant.
¹⁰ For this is the covenant
that I will make with the house of Israel
after those days, says the Lord:
I will put my laws into their minds
and write them on their hearts.
I will be their God,
and they will be my people.
¹¹ And each person will not teach his fellow citizen,
and each his brother or sister, saying, "Know the Lord,"
because they will all know me,
from the least to the greatest of them.
¹² For I will forgive their wrongdoing,
and I will never again remember their sins.

DATE

"Do not be afraid of them, for I have handed them over to you."

JOSHUA 10:8

The Day the Sun Stood Still

Joshua 9
DECEPTION BY GIBEON

¹ When all the kings heard about Jericho and Ai, those who were west of the Jordan in the hill country, in the Judean foothills, and all along the coast of the Mediterranean Sea toward Lebanon—the Hethites, Amorites, Canaanites, Perizzites, Hivites, and Jebusites— ² they formed a unified alliance to fight against Joshua and Israel.

³ When the inhabitants of Gibeon heard what Joshua had done to Jericho and Ai, ⁴ they acted deceptively. They gathered provisions and took worn-out sacks on their donkeys and old wineskins, cracked and mended. ⁵ They wore old, patched sandals on their feet and threadbare clothing on their bodies. Their entire provision of bread was dry and crumbly. ⁶ They went to Joshua in the camp at Gilgal and said to him and the men of Israel, "We have come from a distant land. Please make a treaty with us."

⁷ The men of Israel replied to the Hivites, "Perhaps you live among us. How can we make a treaty with you?"

⁸ They said to Joshua, "We are your servants."

Then Joshua asked them, "Who are you and where do you come from?"

⁹ They replied to him, "Your servants have come from a faraway land because of the reputation of the LORD your God. For we have heard of his fame, and all that he did in Egypt, ¹⁰ and all that he did to the two Amorite kings beyond the Jordan—King Sihon of Heshbon and King Og of Bashan, who was in Ashtaroth. ¹¹ So our elders and all the inhabitants of our land told us, 'Take provisions with you for the journey; go and meet them and say, "We are your servants. Please make a treaty with us."' ¹² This bread of ours was warm when we took it from our houses as food on the day we left to come to you; but see, it is now dry and crumbly. ¹³ These wineskins were new when we filled them; but see, they are cracked. And these clothes and sandals of ours are worn out from the extremely long journey." ¹⁴ Then the men of Israel took some of their provisions, but did not seek the LORD's decision. ¹⁵ So Joshua established peace with them and made a treaty to let them live, and the leaders of the community swore an oath to them.

GIBEON'S DECEPTION DISCOVERED

¹⁶ Three days after making the treaty with them, they heard that the Gibeonites were their neighbors, living among them. ¹⁷ So the Israelites set out and reached the Gibeonite cities on the third day. Now their cities were Gibeon, Chephirah, Beeroth, and Kiriath-jearim. ¹⁸ But the Israelites did not attack them, because the leaders of the community had sworn an oath to them by the LORD, the God of Israel. Then the whole community grumbled against the leaders.

¹⁹ All the leaders answered them, "We have sworn an oath to them by the LORD, the God of Israel, and now we cannot touch them. ²⁰ This is how we will treat them: we will let them live, so that no wrath will fall on us because of the oath we swore to them." ²¹ They also said, "Let them live." So the Gibeonites became woodcutters and water carriers for the whole community, as the leaders had promised them.

²² Joshua summoned the Gibeonites and said to them, "Why did you deceive us by telling us you live far away from us, when in fact you live among us? ²³ Therefore you are cursed and will always be slaves—woodcutters and water carriers for the house of my God."

²⁴ The Gibeonites answered him, "It was clearly communicated to your servants that the LORD your God had commanded his servant Moses to give you all the land and to destroy all the inhabitants of the land before you. We greatly feared for our lives because of you, and that is why we did this. ²⁵ Now we are in your hands. Do to us whatever you think is right." ²⁶ This is what Joshua did to them: he rescued them from the Israelites, and they did not kill them. ²⁷ On that day he made them woodcutters and water carriers—as they are today—for the community and for the LORD's altar at the place he would choose.

Joshua 10:1–15
THE DAY THE SUN STOOD STILL

¹ Now King Adoni-zedek of Jerusalem heard that Joshua had captured Ai and completely destroyed it, treating Ai and its king as he had Jericho and its king, and that the inhabitants of Gibeon had made peace with Israel and were living among them. ² So Adoni-zedek and his people were greatly alarmed because Gibeon was a large city like one of the royal cities; it was larger than Ai, and all its men were warriors. ³ Therefore King Adoni-zedek of Jerusalem sent word to King Hoham of Hebron, King Piram of Jarmuth, King Japhia of Lachish, and King Debir of Eglon, saying, ⁴ "Come up and help me. We will attack Gibeon, because they have made peace with Joshua and the Israelites." ⁵ So the five Amorite kings—the kings of Jerusalem, Hebron, Jarmuth, Lachish, and Eglon—joined forces, advanced with all their armies, besieged Gibeon, and fought against it.

⁶ Then the men of Gibeon sent word to Joshua in the camp at Gilgal: "Don't give up on your servants. Come quickly and save us! Help us, for all the Amorite kings living in the hill country have joined forces against us." ⁷ So Joshua and all his troops, including all his best soldiers, came from Gilgal.

⁸ The LORD said to Joshua, "Do not be afraid of them, for I have handed them over to you. Not one of them will be able to stand against you."

⁹ So Joshua caught them by surprise, after marching all night from Gilgal. ¹⁰ The LORD threw them into confusion before Israel. He defeated them in a great slaughter at Gibeon,

chased them through the ascent of Beth-horon, and struck them down as far as Azekah and Makkedah. ¹¹ As they fled before Israel, the LORD threw large hailstones on them from the sky along the descent of Beth-horon all the way to Azekah, and they died. More of them died from the hail than the Israelites killed with the sword.

¹² On the day the LORD gave the Amorites over to the Israelites, Joshua spoke to the LORD in the presence of Israel:

"Sun, stand still over Gibeon,
and moon, over the Valley of Aijalon."
¹³ And the sun stood still
and the moon stopped
until the nation took vengeance on its enemies.

Isn't this written in the Book of Jashar?

So the sun stopped
in the middle of the sky
and delayed its setting
almost a full day.

¹⁴ There has been no day like it before or since, when the LORD listened to a man, because the LORD fought for Israel.

¹⁵ Then Joshua and all Israel with him returned to the camp at Gilgal.

Psalm 84:10
Better a day in your courts
than a thousand anywhere else.
I would rather stand at the threshold of the house of my God
than live in the tents of wicked people.

God Gives Israel the Land

Joshua 10:16–43
EXECUTION OF THE FIVE KINGS

[16] Now the five defeated kings had fled and hidden in the cave at Makkedah. [17] It was reported to Joshua, "The five kings have been found; they are hiding in the cave at Makkedah."

[18] Joshua said, "Roll large stones against the mouth of the cave, and station men by it to guard the kings. [19] But as for the rest of you, don't stay there. Pursue your enemies and attack them from behind. Don't let them enter their cities, for the Lord your God has handed them over to you." [20] So Joshua and the Israelites finished inflicting a terrible slaughter on them until they were destroyed, although a few survivors ran away to the fortified cities. [21] The people returned safely to Joshua in the camp at Makkedah. And no one dared to threaten the Israelites.

[22] Then Joshua said, "Open the mouth of the cave, and bring those five kings to me out of there." [23] That is what they did. They brought the five kings of Jerusalem, Hebron, Jarmuth, Lachish, and Eglon to Joshua out of the cave. [24] When they had brought the kings to him, Joshua summoned all the men of Israel and said to the military commanders who had accompanied him, "Come here and put your feet on the necks of these

kings." So the commanders came forward and put their feet on their necks. 25 Joshua said to them, "Do not be afraid or discouraged. Be strong and courageous, for the LORD will do this to all the enemies you fight."

26 After this, Joshua struck them down and executed them. He hung their bodies on five trees and they were there until evening. 27 At sunset Joshua commanded that they be taken down from the trees and thrown into the cave where they had hidden. Then large stones were placed against the mouth of the cave, and the stones are still there today.

CONQUEST OF SOUTHERN CITIES

28 On that day Joshua captured Makkedah and struck it down with the sword, including its king. He completely destroyed it and everyone in it, leaving no survivors. So he treated the king of Makkedah as he had the king of Jericho.

29 Joshua and all Israel with him crossed from Makkedah to Libnah and fought against Libnah. 30 The LORD also handed it and its king over to Israel. He struck it down, putting everyone in it to the sword, and left no survivors in it. He treated Libnah's king as he had the king of Jericho.

31 From Libnah, Joshua and all Israel with him crossed to Lachish. They laid siege to it and attacked it. 32 The LORD handed Lachish over to Israel, and Joshua captured it on the second day. He struck it down, putting everyone in it to the sword, just as he had done to Libnah. 33 At that time King Horam of Gezer went to help Lachish, but Joshua struck him down along with his people, leaving no survivors.

34 Then Joshua crossed from Lachish to Eglon and all Israel with him. They laid siege to it and attacked it. 35 On that day they captured it and struck it down, putting everyone in it to the sword. He completely destroyed it that day, just as he had done to Lachish.

36 Next, Joshua and all Israel with him went up from Eglon to Hebron and attacked it. 37 They captured it and struck down its king, all its villages, and everyone in it with the sword. He left no survivors, just as he had done at Eglon. He completely destroyed Hebron and everyone in it.

38 Finally, Joshua turned toward Debir and attacked it. And all Israel was with him. 39 He captured it—its king and all its villages. They struck them down with the sword and completely destroyed everyone in it, leaving no survivors. He treated Debir and its king as he had treated Hebron and as he had treated Libnah and its king.

40 So Joshua conquered the whole region—the hill country, the Negev, the Judean foothills, and the slopes—with all their kings, leaving no survivors. He completely destroyed every living being, as the LORD, the God of Israel, had commanded. 41 Joshua conquered everyone from Kadesh-barnea to Gaza, and all the land of Goshen as far as Gibeon.

42 Joshua captured all these kings and their land in one campaign, because the LORD, the God of Israel, fought for Israel.

43 Then Joshua returned with all Israel to the camp at Gilgal.

Romans 1:18–20

18 For God's wrath is revealed from heaven against all godlessness and unrighteousness of people who by their unrighteousness suppress the truth, 19 since what can be known about God is evident among them, because God has shown it to them. 20 For his invisible attributes, that is, his eternal power and divine nature, have been clearly seen since the creation of the world, being understood through what he has made. As a result, people are without excuse.

Ephesians 1:20–21

20 He exercised this power in Christ by raising him from the dead and seating him at his right hand in the heavens— 21 far above every ruler and authority, power and dominion, and every title given, not only in this age but also in the one to come.

DATE

Great Is Thy Faithfulness

WORDS:
Thomas O. Chisholm

MUSIC:
William M. Runyan

HYMN

1. Great is Thy faith - ful - ness, O God, my Fa - ther; There is no
2. Sum - mer and win - ter, and spring - time and har - vest, Sun, moon and
3. Par - don for sin and a peace that en - dur - eth, Thine own dear

shad - ow of turn - ing with Thee. Thou chang - est not, Thy com -
stars in their cours - es a - bove join with all na - ture in
pres - ence to cheer and to guide; Strength for to - day and bright

pas - sions, they fail not; As Thou hast been, Thou for - ev - er wilt be.
man - i - fold wit - ness to Thy great faith - ful - ness, mer - cy and love.
hope for to - mor - row, Bless - ings all mine with ten thou - sand be - side!

Great is Thy faithfulness, O God, my Father;
There is no shadow of turning with Thee.
Thou changest not, Thy compassions, they fail not;
As Thou hast been, Thou forever wilt be.

Chorus:
Great is Thy faithfulness!
Great is Thy faithfulness!
Morning by morning new mercies I see;
All I have needed Thy hand hath provided;
Great is Thy faithfulness, Lord, unto me!

Summer and winter, and springtime and harvest,
Sun, moon and stars in their courses above
join with all nature in manifold witness
to Thy great faithfulness, mercy and love.

Chorus

Pardon for sin and a peace that endureth,
Thine own dear presence to cheer and to guide;
Strength for today and bright hope for tomorrow,
Blessings all mine with ten thousand beside!

Chorus

So Joshua took the entire land, in keeping with all that the LORD had told Moses.

JOSHUA 11:23

A Battle Without Mercy

Joshua 11
CONQUEST OF NORTHERN CITIES

1 When King Jabin of Hazor heard this news, he sent a message to: King Jobab of Madon, the kings of Shimron and Achshaph, 2 and the kings of the north in the hill country, the Arabah south of Chinnereth, the Judean foothills, and the Slopes of Dor to the west, 3 the Canaanites in the east and west, the Amorites, Hethites, Perizzites, and Jebusites in the hill country, and the Hivites at the foot of Hermon in the land of Mizpah. 4 They went out with all their armies—a multitude as numerous as the sand on the seashore—along with a vast number of horses and chariots. 5 All these kings joined forces; they came and camped together at the Waters of Merom to attack Israel.

6 The LORD said to Joshua, "Do not be afraid of them, for at this time tomorrow I will cause all of them to be killed before Israel. You are to hamstring their horses and burn their chariots." 7 So Joshua and all his troops surprised them at the Waters of Merom and attacked them. 8 The LORD handed them over to Israel, and they struck them down, pursuing them as far as greater Sidon and Misrephoth-maim, and to

the east as far as the Valley of Mizpeh. They struck them down, leaving no survivors. 9 Joshua treated them as the LORD had told him; he hamstrung their horses and burned their chariots.

10 At that time Joshua turned back, captured Hazor, and struck down its king with the sword, because Hazor had formerly been the leader of all these kingdoms. 11 They struck down everyone in it with the sword, completely destroying them; he left no one alive. Then he burned Hazor.

12 Joshua captured all these kings and their cities and struck them down with the sword. He completely destroyed them, as Moses the LORD's servant had commanded. 13 However, Israel did not burn any of the cities that stood on their mounds except Hazor, which Joshua burned. 14 The Israelites plundered all the spoils and cattle of these cities for themselves. But they struck down every person with the sword until they had annihilated them, leaving no one alive. 15 Just as the LORD had commanded his servant Moses,

Moses commanded Joshua. That is what Joshua did, leaving nothing undone of all that the LORD had commanded Moses.

SUMMARY OF CONQUESTS

16 So Joshua took all this land—the hill country, all the Negev, all the land of Goshen, the foothills, the Arabah, and the hill country of Israel with its foothills— 17 from Mount Halak, which ascends to Seir, as far as Baal-gad in the Valley of Lebanon at the foot of Mount Hermon. He captured all their kings and struck them down, putting them to death. 18 Joshua waged war with all these kings for a long time. 19 No city made peace with the Israelites except the Hivites who inhabited Gibeon; all of them were taken in battle. 20 For it was the LORD's intention to harden their hearts, so that they would engage Israel in battle, be completely destroyed without mercy, and be annihilated, just as the LORD had commanded Moses.

21 At that time Joshua proceeded to exterminate the Anakim from the hill country—Hebron, Debir, Anab—all the hill country of Judah and of Israel. Joshua completely destroyed them with their cities. 22 No Anakim were left in the land of the Israelites, except for some remaining in Gaza, Gath, and Ashdod.

23 So Joshua took the entire land, in keeping with all that the LORD had told Moses. Joshua then gave it as an inheritance to Israel according to their tribal allotments. After this, the land had rest from war.

Psalm 110
THE PRIESTLY KING

A psalm of David.

1 This is the declaration of the LORD
to my Lord:
"Sit at my right hand
until I make your enemies your footstool."
2 The LORD will extend your mighty scepter from Zion.
Rule over your surrounding enemies.
3 Your people will volunteer
on your day of battle.
In holy splendor, from the womb of the dawn,
the dew of your youth belongs to you.

4 The LORD has sworn an oath and will not take it back:
"You are a priest forever
according to the pattern of Melchizedek."

5 The Lord is at your right hand;
he will crush kings on the day of his anger.
6 He will judge the nations, heaping up corpses;
he will crush leaders over the entire world.
7 He will drink from the brook by the road;
therefore, he will lift up his head.

Ephesians 1:3–14
GOD'S RICH BLESSINGS

3 Blessed is the God and Father of our Lord Jesus Christ, who has blessed us with every spiritual blessing in the heavens in Christ. 4 For he chose us in him, before the foundation of the world, to be holy and blameless in love before him. 5 He predestined us to be adopted as sons through Jesus Christ for himself, according to the good pleasure of his will, 6 to the praise of his glorious grace that he lavished on us in the Beloved One.

7 In him we have redemption through his blood, the forgiveness of our trespasses, according to the riches of his grace 8 that he richly poured out on us with all wisdom and understanding. 9 He made known to us the mystery of his will, according to his good pleasure that he purposed in Christ 10 as a plan for the right time—to bring everything together in Christ, both things in heaven and things on earth in him.

11 In him we have also received an inheritance, because we were predestined according to the plan of the one who works out everything in agreement with the purpose of his will, 12 so that we who had already put our hope in Christ might bring praise to his glory.

13 In him you also were sealed with the promised Holy Spirit when you heard the word of truth, the gospel of your salvation, and when you believed. 14 The Holy Spirit is the down payment of our inheritance, until the redemption of the possession, to the praise of his glory.

DATE

REFLECT & REMEMBER

In Joshua, stones or stone altars were often used to mark places where God's presence was evident or to memorialize fulfilled promises. Joshua 4 includes a detailed account of how the use of memorial stones helped God's people remember His faithfulness. We, too, are called to remember and proclaim God's work in our lives (2Pt 1:12).

"So if the Son sets you free, you really will be free."

JOHN 8:36

Use this journaling space to reflect on a time when God freed you from an unhealthy situation or behavior. Let this written account be your personal stone of remembrance to mark God's work in your life for you to look back on in the days to come.

DAY 13: GRACE DAY

*Take this day to catch up on
your reading, pray, and rest in
the presence of the Lord.*

Better a day in your courts than a thousand anywhere else.

PSALM 84:10

WEEKLY

DAY 14

Scripture is God-breathed and true. When we memorize it, we carry His Word with us wherever we go.

This week, we will memorize the second part of Joshua 1:9. Continue reading the full verse out loud three times, and practice your memorization by underlining or highlighting certain words as you copy them down.

"Haven't I commanded you: be strong and courageous?

Do not be afraid or discouraged,

for the LORD your God is with you wherever you go."

JOSHUA 1:9

And Moses the Lord's servant gave their land as an inheritance to the Reubenites…

JOSHUA 12:6

Territories & Kings

Joshua 12
TERRITORY EAST OF THE JORDAN

¹ The Israelites struck down the following kings of the land and took possession of their land beyond the Jordan to the east and from the Arnon River to Mount Hermon, including all the Arabah eastward:

² King Sihon of the Amorites lived in Heshbon. He ruled from Aroer on the rim of the Arnon River, along the middle of the valley, and half of Gilead up to the Jabbok River (the border of the Ammonites), ³ the Arabah east of the Sea of Chinnereth to the Sea of Arabah (that is, the Dead Sea), eastward through Beth-jeshimoth and southward below the slopes of Pisgah.

⁴ King Og of Bashan, of the remnant of the Rephaim, lived in Ashtaroth and Edrei. ⁵ He ruled over Mount Hermon, Salecah, all Bashan up to the Geshurite and Maacathite border, and half of Gilead to the border of King Sihon of Heshbon. ⁶ Moses the LORD's servant and the Israelites struck them down. And Moses the LORD's servant gave their land as an inheritance to the Reubenites, Gadites, and half the tribe of Manasseh.

⁷ Joshua and the Israelites struck down the following kings of the land beyond the Jordan to the west, from Baal-gad in the Valley of Lebanon to Mount Halak, which ascends toward Seir (Joshua gave their land as an inheritance to the tribes of Israel according to their allotments: ⁸ the hill country, the Judean foothills, the Arabah, the slopes, the wilderness, and the Negev—the lands of the Hethites, Amorites, Canaanites, Perizzites, Hivites, and Jebusites):

⁹ the king of Jericho	one
the king of Ai, which is next to Bethel	one
¹⁰ the king of Jerusalem	one
the king of Hebron	one
¹¹ the king of Jarmuth	one
the king of Lachish	one
¹² the king of Eglon	one
the king of Gezer	one
¹³ the king of Debir	one
the king of Geder	one
¹⁴ the king of Hormah	one
the king of Arad	one
¹⁵ the king of Libnah	one
the king of Adullam	one
¹⁶ the king of Makkedah	one
the king of Bethel	one
¹⁷ the king of Tappuah	one
the king of Hepher	one
¹⁸ the king of Aphek	one
the king of Lasharon	one
¹⁹ the king of Madon	one
the king of Hazor	one
²⁰ the king of Shimron-meron	one
the king of Achshaph	one
²¹ the king of Taanach	one
the king of Megiddo	one
²² the king of Kedesh	one
the king of Jokneam in Carmel	one
²³ the king of Dor in Naphath-dor	one
the king of Goiim in Gilgal	one
²⁴ the king of Tirzah	one
the total number of all kings:	thirty-one.

Nehemiah 9:22

You gave them kingdoms and peoples
and established boundaries for them.
They took possession
of the land of King Sihon of Heshbon
and of the land of King Og of Bashan.

Psalm 136:16–21

¹⁶ He led his people in the wilderness.
  His faithful love endures forever.
¹⁷ He struck down great kings
  His faithful love endures forever.
¹⁸ and slaughtered famous kings—
  His faithful love endures forever.
¹⁹ Sihon king of the Amorites
  His faithful love endures forever.
²⁰ and Og king of Bashan—
  His faithful love endures forever.
²¹ and gave their land as an inheritance,
  His faithful love endures forever.

Daniel 2:19–22

¹⁹ The mystery was then revealed to Daniel in a vision at night, and Daniel praised the God of the heavens ²⁰ and declared:

May the name of God
be praised forever and ever,
for wisdom and power belong to him.
²¹ He changes the times and seasons;
he removes kings and establishes kings.
He gives wisdom to the wise
and knowledge to those
who have understanding.
²² He reveals the deep and hidden things;
he knows what is in the darkness,
and light dwells with him.

DATE

Unconquered Lands

Joshua 13
UNCONQUERED LANDS

¹ Joshua was now old, advanced in age, and the LORD said to him, "You have become old, advanced in age, but a great deal of the land remains to be possessed. ² This is the land that remains:

All the districts of the Philistines and the Geshurites: ³ from the Shihor east of Egypt to the border of Ekron on the north (considered to be Canaanite territory)—the five Philistine rulers of Gaza, Ashdod, Ashkelon, Gath, and Ekron, as well as the Avvites ⁴ in the south; all the land of the Canaanites, from Arah of the Sidonians to Aphek and as far as the border of the Amorites; ⁵ the land of the Gebalites; and all Lebanon east from Baal-gad below Mount Hermon to the entrance of Hamath— ⁶ all the inhabitants of the hill country from Lebanon to Misrephoth-maim, all the Sidonians.

I will drive them out before the Israelites, only distribute the land as an inheritance for Israel, as I have commanded you.

⁷ Therefore, divide this land as an inheritance to the nine tribes and half the tribe of Manasseh."

THE INHERITANCE EAST OF THE JORDAN

⁸ With the other half of the tribe of Manasseh, the Reubenites and Gadites had received the inheritance Moses gave them beyond the Jordan to the east, just as Moses the LORD's servant had given them:

⁹ From Aroer on the rim of the Arnon Valley, along with the city in the middle of the valley, all the Medeba plateau as far as Dibon, ¹⁰ and all the cities of King Sihon of the Amorites, who reigned in Heshbon, to the border of the Ammonites; ¹¹ also Gilead and the territory of the Geshurites and Maacathites, all Mount Hermon, and all Bashan to Salecah— ¹² the whole kingdom of Og in Bashan, who reigned in Ashtaroth and Edrei; he was one of the remaining Rephaim.

Moses struck them down and drove them out, [13] but the Israelites did not drive out the Geshurites and Maacathites. So Geshur and Maacath still live in Israel today.

[14] He did not, however, give any inheritance to the tribe of Levi. This was their inheritance, just as he had promised: the food offerings made to the LORD, the God of Israel.

REUBEN'S INHERITANCE

[15] To the tribe of Reuben's descendants by their clans, Moses gave [16] this as their territory:

From Aroer on the rim of the Arnon Valley, along with the city in the middle of the valley, the whole plateau as far as Medeba, [17] with Heshbon and all its cities on the plateau—Dibon, Bamoth-baal, Beth-baal-meon, [18] Jahaz, Kedemoth, Mephaath, [19] Kiriathaim, Sibmah, Zereth-shahar on the hill in the valley, [20] Beth-peor, the slopes of Pisgah, and Beth-jeshimoth— [21] all the cities of the plateau, and all the kingdom of King Sihon of the Amorites, who reigned in Heshbon. Moses had killed him and the chiefs of Midian—Evi, Rekem, Zur, Hur, and Reba—the princes of Sihon who lived in the land. [22] Along with those the Israelites put to death, they also killed the diviner, Balaam son of Beor, with the sword.

[23] The border of the Reubenites was the Jordan and its plain. This was the inheritance of the Reubenites by their clans, with the cities and their settlements.

GAD'S INHERITANCE

[24] To the tribe of the Gadites by their clans, Moses gave [25] this as their territory:

Jazer and all the cities of Gilead, and half the land of the Ammonites to Aroer, near Rabbah; [26] from Heshbon to Ramath-mizpeh and Betonim, and from Mahanaim to the border of Debir; [27] in the valley: Beth-haram, Beth-nimrah, Succoth, and Zaphon—the rest of the kingdom of King Sihon of Heshbon. Their land also included the Jordan and its territory as far as the edge of the Sea of Chinnereth on the east side of the Jordan.

[28] This was the inheritance of the Gadites by their clans, with the cities and their settlements.

EAST MANASSEH'S INHERITANCE

[29] And to half the tribe of Manasseh (that is, to half the tribe of Manasseh's descendants by their clans) Moses gave [30] this as their territory:

From Mahanaim through all Bashan—all the kingdom of King Og of Bashan, including all of Jair's Villages that are in Bashan—sixty cities. [31] But half of Gilead, and Og's royal cities in Bashan—Ashtaroth and Edrei—are for the descendants of Machir son of Manasseh (that is, half the descendants of Machir by their clans).

[32] These were the portions Moses gave them on the plains of Moab beyond the Jordan east of Jericho. [33] But Moses did not give a portion to the tribe of Levi. The LORD, the God of Israel, was their inheritance, just as he had promised them.

Deuteronomy 3:22

Don't be afraid of them, for the LORD your God fights for you.

Revelation 5:9–10

[9] And they sang a new song:

You are worthy to take the scroll
and to open its seals,
because you were slaughtered,
and you purchased people
for God by your blood
from every tribe and language
and people and nation.
[10] You made them a kingdom
and priests to our God,
and they will reign on the earth.

DATE

Caleb's Loyalty to God

DAY 17

Joshua 14
Numbers 14:1–25
Romans 11:33–36

MOUNT OF BEATITUDES · NAPHTALI

Joshua 14
ISRAEL'S INHERITANCE IN CANAAN

¹ The Israelites received these portions that the priest Eleazar, Joshua son of Nun, and the family heads of the Israelite tribes gave them in the land of Canaan. ² Their inheritance was by lot as the LORD commanded through Moses for the nine and a half tribes, ³ because Moses had given the inheritance to the two and a half tribes beyond the Jordan. But he gave no inheritance among them to the Levites. ⁴ The descendants of Joseph became two tribes, Manasseh and Ephraim. No portion of the land was given to the Levites except cities to live in, along with pasturelands for their cattle and livestock. ⁵ So the Israelites did as the LORD commanded Moses, and they divided the land.

CALEB'S INHERITANCE

⁶ The descendants of Judah approached Joshua at Gilgal, and Caleb son of Jephunneh the Kenizzite said to him, "You know what the LORD promised Moses the man of God at Kadesh-barnea about you and me. ⁷ I was forty years old when Moses the LORD's servant sent me from Kadesh-barnea to scout the land, and I brought back an honest report. ⁸ My brothers who went with me caused the people to lose heart, but I followed the LORD my God completely. ⁹ On that day Moses swore to me, 'The land where you have set foot will be an inheritance for you and your descendants forever, because you have followed the LORD my God completely.'

¹⁰ "As you see, the LORD has kept me alive these forty-five years as he promised, since the LORD spoke this word to Moses while Israel was journeying in the wilderness. Here I am today, eighty-five years old. ¹¹ I am still as strong today as I was the day Moses sent me out. My strength for battle and for daily tasks is now as it was then. ¹² Now give me this hill country the LORD promised me on that day, because you heard then that the Anakim are there, as well as large fortified cities. Perhaps the LORD will be with me and I will drive them out as the LORD promised."

¹³ Then Joshua blessed Caleb son of Jephunneh and gave him Hebron as an inheritance. ¹⁴ Therefore, Hebron still belongs to Caleb son of Jephunneh the Kenizzite as an inheritance today because he followed the LORD, the God of Israel, completely. ¹⁵ Hebron's name used to be Kiriath-arba; Arba was the greatest man among the Anakim. After this, the land had rest from war.

Numbers 14:1–25
ISRAEL'S REFUSAL TO ENTER CANAAN

¹ Then the whole community broke into loud cries, and the people wept that night. ² All the Israelites complained about Moses and Aaron, and the whole community told them, "If only we had died in the land of Egypt, or if only we had died in this wilderness! ³ Why is the LORD bringing us into this land to die by the sword? Our wives and children will become plunder. Wouldn't it be better for us to go back to Egypt?" ⁴ So they said to one another, "Let's appoint a leader and go back to Egypt."

⁵ Then Moses and Aaron fell facedown in front of the whole assembly of the Israelite community. ⁶ Joshua son of Nun and Caleb son of Jephunneh, who were among those who scouted out the land, tore their clothes ⁷ and said to the entire Israelite community, "The land we passed through and explored is an extremely good land. ⁸ If the LORD is pleased with us, he will bring us into this land, a land flowing with milk and honey, and give it to us. ⁹ Only don't rebel against the LORD, and don't be afraid of the people of the land, for we will devour them. Their protection has been removed from them, and the LORD is with us. Don't be afraid of them!"

¹⁰ While the whole community threatened to stone them, the glory of the LORD appeared to all the Israelites at the tent of meeting.

GOD'S JUDGMENT OF ISRAEL'S REBELLION

¹¹ The LORD said to Moses, "How long will these people despise me? How long will they not trust in me despite all the signs I have performed among them? ¹² I will strike them with a plague and destroy them. Then I will make you into a greater and mightier nation than they are."

¹³ But Moses replied to the LORD, "The Egyptians will hear about it, for by your strength you brought up this people from them. ¹⁴ They will tell it to the inhabitants of this land. They have heard that you, LORD, are among these people,

how you, Lord, are seen face to face, how your cloud stands over them, and how you go before them in a pillar of cloud by day and in a pillar of fire by night. [15] If you kill this people with a single blow, the nations that have heard of your fame will declare, [16] 'Since the Lord wasn't able to bring this people into the land he swore to give them, he has slaughtered them in the wilderness.'

[17] "So now, may my Lord's power be magnified just as you have spoken: [18] The Lord is slow to anger and abounding in faithful love, forgiving iniquity and rebellion. But he will not leave the guilty unpunished, bringing the consequences of the fathers' iniquity on the children to the third and fourth generation. [19] Please pardon the iniquity of this people, in keeping with the greatness of your faithful love, just as you have forgiven them from Egypt until now."

[20] The Lord responded, "I have pardoned them as you requested. [21] Yet as I live and as the whole earth is filled with the Lord's glory, [22] none of the men who have seen my glory and the signs I performed in Egypt and in the wilderness, and have tested me these ten times and did not obey me, [23] will ever see the land I swore to give their ancestors. None of those who have despised me will see it.

[24] But since my servant Caleb has a different spirit and has remained loyal to me, I will bring him into the land where he has gone, and his descendants will inherit it.

[25] Since the Amalekites and Canaanites are living in the lowlands, turn back tomorrow and head for the wilderness in the direction of the Red Sea."

Romans 11:33–36
A HYMN OF PRAISE

[33] Oh, the depth of the riches
and the wisdom and the knowledge of God!
How unsearchable his judgments
and untraceable his ways!
[34] For who has known the mind of the Lord?
Or who has been his counselor?
[35] And who has ever given to God,
that he should be repaid?
[36] For from him and through him
and to him are all things.
To him be the glory forever. Amen.

DATE

MAP

The Twelve Tribes of Israel

ASHER **8**

NAPHTALI **6**

EAST MANASSEH **11**

Sea of Galilee

ZEBULUN **10**

▲ Mt. Carmel

● Nazareth

ISSACHAR **9**

LEVI **3**

WEST MANASSEH **11**

Jordan River

Mediterranean Sea

EPHRAIM **11**

● Tel Aviv

● Jaffa

BENJAMIN **12**

GAD **7**

JORDAN

DAN **5**

Mt. of Olives ▲

● Jerusalem

▲ Mt. Nebo

● Bethlehem

REUBEN **1**

JUDAH **4**

GAZA STRIP

Dead Sea

SIMEON **2**

ORIGINAL TRIBAL BOUNDARIES

MODERN BOUNDARIES

● FUTURE SITES OF ISRAELI CITIES
for reference

EGYPT

MI 10 20 30 40
KM 20 40 60

"As for me, here is my covenant with you: You will become the father of many nations...I will make you extremely fruitful and will make nations and kings come from you. I will confirm my covenant that is between me and you and your future offspring throughout their generations. It is a permanent covenant to be your God and the God of your offspring after you. And to you and your future offspring I will give the land where you are residing—all the land of Canaan—as a permanent possession, and I will be their God."

GENESIS 17:4–8

God's promise to Abraham in Genesis marked the beginning of a unique relationship between God and Abraham's descendants through his son Isaac. In Genesis 32 and 35, God met with Abraham's grandson Jacob and renamed him Israel. These encounters affirmed that God's covenant would be fulfilled through Jacob's lineage, the eponymous nation of Israel. Through Jacob's twelve sons, this family would grow into a large nation of many tribes that Joshua would lead into the land promised to Abraham.

This list below shows the relationship between the tribal allotments found in the second half of Joshua, and Jacob's twelve sons. These sons are listed here in order of their birth, along with the name each son was given by his mother to commemorate the circumstances of his birth.

1 - - - - - - **2** - - - - - - **3** - - - - - - **4** - - - - - -

Reuben
SON OF LEAH

Meaning
The LORD has seen my affliction. **GN 29:32**

Simeon
SON OF LEAH

Meaning
The LORD heard. **GN 29:33**

Levi
SON OF LEAH

Meaning
My husband will become attached to me. **GN 29:34**

Because the tribe of Levi functioned as priests, they did not receive a geographical tribal allotment. However, God commanded the other tribes to give the Levites forty-eight cities from their territories to live in and raise livestock. God also commanded that a portion of all offerings and other sacrifices be given to the Levites as an inheritance.

Judah
SON OF LEAH

Meaning
I will praise the LORD. **GN 29:35**

⑤ Dan

SON OF BILHAH,
RACHEL'S HANDMAID

Meaning
God has vindicated me.
GN 30:6

⑥ Naphtali

SON OF BILHAH,
RACHEL'S HANDMAID

Meaning
I have wrestled. GN 30:8

⑦ Gad

SON OF ZILPAH,
LEAH'S HANDMAID

Meaning
What good fortune!
GN 30:11

⑧ Asher

SON OF ZILPAH,
LEAH'S HANDMAID

Meaning
I am happy. GN 30:13

(9)

Issachar

SON OF LEAH

Meaning
God has rewarded me.
GN 30:18

(10)

Zebulun

SON OF LEAH

Meaning
My husband will honor me.
GN 30:20

(11)

Joseph

SON OF RACHEL

Meaning
May the LORD add another
son to me. GN 30:24

The tribes of Manasseh and
Ephraim, named for Joseph's
two sons, are treated as
tribes of Joseph. Manasseh
is also sometimes referred to
as a half-tribe, because half
of the tribe was given land
on the east side of the Jordan
River and the other half the
land west of the Jordan.

(12)

Benjamin

SON OF RACHEL

Meaning
She named him Ben-oni,
but his father called him
Benjamin. GN 35:18

Judah's Inheritance

Joshua 15
JUDAH'S INHERITANCE

[1] Now the allotment for the tribe of the descendants of Judah by their clans was in the southernmost region, south to the Wilderness of Zin and over to the border of Edom.

[2] Their southern border began at the tip of the Dead Sea on the south bay [3] and went south of the Scorpions' Ascent, proceeded to Zin, ascended to the south of Kadesh-barnea, passed Hezron, ascended to Addar, and turned to Karka. [4] It proceeded to Azmon and to the Brook of Egypt and so the border ended at the Mediterranean Sea. This is your southern border.

[5] Now the eastern border was along the Dead Sea to the mouth of the Jordan.

The border on the north side was from the bay of the sea at the mouth of the Jordan. [6] It ascended to Beth-hoglah, proceeded north of Beth-arabah, and ascended to the Stone of Bohan son of Reuben. [7] Then the border ascended to Debir from the Valley of Achor, turning north to the Gilgal that is opposite the Ascent of Adummim, which is south of the ravine. The border proceeded to the Waters of En-shemesh and ended at En-rogel. [8] From there the border ascended Ben Hinnom Valley to the southern Jebusite slope (that is, Jerusalem) and ascended to the top of the hill that faces Hinnom Valley on the west, at the northern end of Rephaim Valley. [9] From the top of the hill the border curved to the spring of the Waters of Nephtoah, went to the cities of Mount Ephron, and then curved to Baalah (that is, Kiriath-jearim). [10] The border turned westward from Baalah to Mount Seir, went to the northern slope of Mount Jearim (that is, Chesalon), descended to Beth-shemesh, and proceeded to Timnah. [11] Then the border reached to the slope north of Ekron, curved to Shikkeron, proceeded to Mount Baalah, went to Jabneel, and ended at the Mediterranean Sea.

[12] Now the western border was the coastline of the Mediterranean Sea.

This was the boundary of the descendants of Judah around their clans.

CALEB AND OTHNIEL

13 He gave Caleb son of Jephunneh the following portion among the descendants of Judah based on the LORD's instruction to Joshua: Kiriath-arba (that is, Hebron; Arba was the father of Anak). 14 Caleb drove out from there the three sons of Anak: Sheshai, Ahiman, and Talmai, descendants of Anak. 15 From there he marched against the inhabitants of Debir, which used to be called Kiriath-sepher, 16 and Caleb said, "Whoever attacks and captures Kiriath-sepher, I will give my daughter Achsah to him as a wife." 17 So Othniel son of Caleb's brother, Kenaz, captured it, and Caleb gave his daughter Achsah to him as a wife. 18 When she arrived, she persuaded Othniel to ask her father for a field. As she got off her donkey, Caleb asked her, "What can I do for you?" 19 She replied, "Give me a blessing. Since you have given me land in the Negev, give me the springs also." So he gave her the upper and lower springs.

JUDAH'S CITIES

20 This was the inheritance of the tribe of the descendants of Judah by their clans.

21 These were the outermost cities of the tribe of the descendants of Judah toward the border of Edom in the Negev: Kabzeel, Eder, Jagur, 22 Kinah, Dimonah, Adadah, 23 Kedesh, Hazor, Ithnan, 24 Ziph, Telem, Bealoth, 25 Hazor-hadattah, Kerioth-hezron (that is, Hazor), 26 Amam, Shema, Moladah, 27 Hazar-gaddah, Heshmon, Beth-pelet, 28 Hazar-shual, Beer-sheba, Biziothiah, 29 Baalah, Iim, Ezem, 30 Eltolad, Chesil, Hormah, 31 Ziklag, Madmannah, Sansannah, 32 Lebaoth, Shilhim, Ain, and Rimmon—twenty-nine cities in all, with their settlements.

33 In the Judean foothills: Eshtaol, Zorah, Ashnah, 34 Zanoah, En-gannim, Tappuah, Enam, 35 Jarmuth, Adullam, Socoh, Azekah, 36 Shaaraim, Adithaim, Gederah, and Gederothaim—fourteen cities, with their settlements; 37 Zenan, Hadashah, Migdal-gad, 38 Dilan, Mizpeh, Jokthe-el, 39 Lachish, Bozkath, Eglon, 40 Cabbon, Lahmam, Chitlish, 41 Gederoth, Beth-dagon, Naamah, and Makkedah—sixteen cities, with their settlements; 42 Libnah, Ether, Ashan, 43 Iphtah, Ashnah, Nezib, 44 Keilah, Achzib, and Mareshah—nine cities, with their settlements; 45 Ekron, with its surrounding villages and settlements; 46 from Ekron to the sea, all the cities near Ashdod, with their settlements; 47 Ashdod, with its surrounding villages and settlements; Gaza, with its surrounding villages and settlements, to the Brook of Egypt and the coastline of the Mediterranean Sea.

48 In the hill country: Shamir, Jattir, Socoh, 49 Dannah, Kiriath-sannah (that is, Debir), 50 Anab, Eshtemoh, Anim, 51 Goshen, Holon, and Giloh—eleven cities, with their settlements; 52 Arab, Dumah, Eshan, 53 Janim, Beth-tappuah, Aphekah, 54 Humtah, Kiriath-arba (that is, Hebron), and Zior—nine cities, with their settlements; 55 Maon, Carmel, Ziph, Juttah, 56 Jezreel, Jokdeam, Zanoah, 57 Kain, Gibeah, and Timnah—ten cities, with their settlements; 58 Halhul, Beth-zur, Gedor, 59 Maarath, Beth-anoth, and Eltekon—six cities, with their settlements; 60 Kiriath-baal (that is, Kiriath-jearim), and Rabbah—two cities, with their settlements.

61 In the wilderness: Beth-arabah, Middin, Secacah, 62 Nibshan, the City of Salt, and En-gedi—six cities, with their settlements.

63 But the descendants of Judah could not drive out the Jebusites who lived in Jerusalem. So the Jebusites still live in Jerusalem among the descendants of Judah today.

Genesis 49:1–27
JACOB'S LAST WORDS

1 Then Jacob called his sons and said, "Gather around, and I will tell you what will happen to you in the days to come.

2 Come together and listen, sons of Jacob;
listen to your father Israel:

3 Reuben, you are my firstborn,
my strength and the firstfruits of my virility,
excelling in prominence, excelling in power.

⁴ Turbulent as water, you will not excel,
because you got into your father's bed
and you defiled it—he got into my bed.

⁵ Simeon and Levi are brothers;
their knives are vicious weapons.
⁶ May I never enter their council;
may I never join their assembly.
For in their anger they kill men,
and on a whim they hamstring oxen.
⁷ Their anger is cursed, for it is strong,
and their fury, for it is cruel!
I will disperse them throughout Jacob
and scatter them throughout Israel.

⁸ Judah, your brothers will praise you.
Your hand will be on the necks of your enemies;
your father's sons will bow down to you.
⁹ Judah is a young lion—
my son, you return from the kill.
He crouches; he lies down like a lion
or a lioness—who dares to rouse him?
¹⁰ The scepter will not depart from Judah
or the staff from between his feet
until he whose right it is comes
and the obedience of the peoples belongs to him.
¹¹ He ties his donkey to a vine,
and the colt of his donkey to the choice vine.
He washes his clothes in wine
and his robes in the blood of grapes.
¹² His eyes are darker than wine,
and his teeth are whiter than milk.

¹³ Zebulun will live by the seashore
and will be a harbor for ships,
and his territory will be next to Sidon.

¹⁴ Issachar is a strong donkey
lying down between the saddlebags.
¹⁵ He saw that his resting place was good
and that the land was pleasant,
so he leaned his shoulder to bear a load
and became a forced laborer.

¹⁶ Dan will judge his people
as one of the tribes of Israel.
¹⁷ Dan will be a snake by the road,
a viper beside the path,
that bites the horse's heels
so that its rider falls backward.

¹⁸ I wait for your salvation, LORD.

¹⁹ Gad will be attacked by raiders,
but he will attack their heels.

²⁰ Asher's food will be rich,
and he will produce royal delicacies.

²¹ Naphtali is a doe set free
that bears beautiful fawns.

²² Joseph is a fruitful vine,
a fruitful vine beside a spring;
its branches climb over the wall.
²³ The archers attacked him,
shot at him, and were hostile toward him.
²⁴ Yet his bow remained steady,
and his strong arms were made agile
by the hands of the Mighty One of Jacob,
by the name of the Shepherd, the Rock of Israel,
²⁵ by the God of your father who helps you,
and by the Almighty who blesses you
with blessings of the heavens above,
blessings of the deep that lies below,
and blessings of the breasts and the womb.
²⁶ The blessings of your father excel
the blessings of my ancestors
and the bounty of the ancient hills.
May they rest on the head of Joseph,
on the brow of the prince of his brothers.

²⁷ Benjamin is a wolf; he tears his prey.
In the morning he devours the prey,
and in the evening he divides the plunder."

John 10:7–10

[7] Jesus said again, "Truly I tell you, I am the gate for the sheep. [8] All who came before me are thieves and robbers, but the sheep didn't listen to them. [9] I am the gate. If anyone enters by me, he will be saved and will come in and go out and find pasture. [10] A thief comes only to steal and kill and destroy.

I have come so that they may have life and have it in abundance."

We have many people, because the LORD has been blessing us greatly.

JOSHUA 17:14

Joseph's Inheritance

Joshua 16
JOSEPH'S INHERITANCE

¹ The allotment for the descendants of Joseph went from the Jordan at Jericho to the Waters of Jericho on the east, through the wilderness ascending from Jericho into the hill country of Bethel. ² From Bethel it went to Luz and proceeded to the border of the Archites by Ataroth. ³ It then descended westward to the border of the Japhletites as far as the border of Lower Beth-horon, then to Gezer, and ended at the Mediterranean Sea. ⁴ So Ephraim and Manasseh, the sons of Joseph, received their inheritance.

EPHRAIM'S INHERITANCE

⁵ This was the territory of the descendants of Ephraim by their clans:

The border of their inheritance went from Ataroth-addar on the east to Upper Beth-horon. ⁶ In the north the border went westward from Michmethath; it turned eastward from Taanath-shiloh and passed it east of Janoah. ⁷ From Janoah it descended to Ataroth and Naarah, and then reached Jericho and went to the Jordan. ⁸ From Tappuah the border went westward along the Brook of Kanah and ended at the Mediterranean Sea.

This was the inheritance of the tribe of the descendants of Ephraim by their clans, together with ⁹ the cities set apart for the descendants of Ephraim within the inheritance of the descendants of Manasseh—all these cities with their settlements. ¹⁰ However, they did not drive out the Canaanites who lived in Gezer. So the Canaanites still live in Ephraim today, but they are forced laborers.

Joshua 17
WEST MANASSEH'S INHERITANCE

¹ This was the allotment for the tribe of Manasseh as Joseph's firstborn. Gilead and Bashan were given to Machir, the firstborn of Manasseh and the father of Gilead, because he was a man of war. ² So the allotment was for the rest

of Manasseh's descendants by their clans, for the sons of Abiezer, Helek, Asriel, Shechem, Hepher, and Shemida. These are the male descendants of Manasseh son of Joseph, by their clans.

³ Now Zelophehad son of Hepher, son of Gilead, son of Machir, son of Manasseh, had no sons, only daughters. These are the names of his daughters: Mahlah, Noah, Hoglah, Milcah, and Tirzah. ⁴ They came before the priest Eleazar, Joshua son of Nun, and the leaders, saying, "The LORD commanded Moses to give us an inheritance among our male relatives."

So they gave them an inheritance among their father's brothers, in keeping with the LORD's instruction.

⁵ As a result, ten tracts fell to Manasseh, besides the land of Gilead and Bashan, which are beyond the Jordan, ⁶ because Manasseh's daughters received an inheritance among his sons. The land of Gilead belonged to the rest of Manasseh's sons.

⁷ The border of Manasseh went from Asher to Michmethath near Shechem. It then went southward toward the inhabitants of En-tappuah. ⁸ The region of Tappuah belonged to Manasseh, but Tappuah itself on Manasseh's border belonged to the descendants of Ephraim. ⁹ From there the border descended to the Brook of Kanah; south of the brook, cities belonged to Ephraim among Manasseh's cities. Manasseh's border was on the north side of the brook and ended at the Mediterranean Sea. ¹⁰ Ephraim's territory was to the south and Manasseh's to the north, with the Sea as its border. They reached Asher on the north and Issachar on the east. ¹¹ Within Issachar and Asher, Manasseh had Beth-shean, Ibleam, and the inhabitants of Dor with their surrounding villages; the inhabitants of En-dor, Taanach, and Megiddo—the three cities of Naphath—with their surrounding villages.

¹² The descendants of Manasseh could not possess these cities, because the Canaanites were determined to stay in this land. ¹³ However, when the Israelites grew stronger, they imposed forced labor on the Canaanites but did not drive them out completely.

JOSEPH'S ADDITIONAL INHERITANCE

¹⁴ Joseph's descendants said to Joshua, "Why did you give us only one tribal allotment as an inheritance? We have many people, because the LORD has been blessing us greatly."

¹⁵ "If you have so many people," Joshua replied to them, "go to the forest and clear an area for yourselves there in the land of the Perizzites and the Rephaim, because Ephraim's hill country is too small for you."

¹⁶ But the descendants of Joseph said, "The hill country is not enough for us, and all the Canaanites who inhabit the valley area have iron chariots, both at Beth-shean with its surrounding villages and in the Jezreel Valley."

¹⁷ So Joshua replied to Joseph's family (that is, Ephraim and Manasseh), "You have many people and great strength. You will not have just one allotment, ¹⁸ because the hill country will be yours also. It is a forest; clear it and its outlying areas will be yours. You can also drive out the Canaanites, even though they have iron chariots and are strong."

Psalm 2:8
Ask of me,
and I will make the nations your inheritance
and the ends of the earth your possession.

1 Peter 1:3–5
A LIVING HOPE

³ Blessed be the God and Father of our Lord Jesus Christ. Because of his great mercy he has given us new birth into a living hope through the resurrection of Jesus Christ from the dead ⁴ and into an inheritance that is imperishable, undefiled, and unfading, kept in heaven for you. ⁵ You are being guarded by God's power through faith for a salvation that is ready to be revealed in the last time.

DATE

REFLECT & REMEMBER

In Joshua, stones or stone altars were often used to mark places where God's presence was evident or to memorialize fulfilled promises. Joshua 4 includes a detailed account of how the use of memorial stones helped God's people remember His faithfulness. We, too, are called to remember and proclaim God's work in our lives (2Pt 1:12).

We know that all things work together for the good of those who love God, who are called according to his purpose.

ROMANS 8:28

Use this journaling space to reflect on a time when God brought unexpected goodness or healing from a broken situation. Let this written account be your personal stone of remembrance to mark God's work in your life for you to look back on in the days to come.

DAY 20: GRACE DAY

*Take this day to catch up on
your reading, pray, and rest in
the presence of the Lord.*

I have come so that they may have life and have it in abundance.

JOHN 10:10

WEEKLY

DAY 21

Scripture is God-breathed and true. When we memorize it, we carry His Word with us wherever we go.

Over the last two weeks, we've worked on memorizing Joshua 1:9. This week, we will memorize the final part of the verse. Repeat the pattern of saying it aloud three times, then writing it out by hand.

"Haven't I commanded you: be strong and courageous?

Do not be afraid or discouraged,

for the Lord your God is with you wherever you go."

JOSHUA 1:9

TRUTH

Joshua Divides the Land

Joshua 18

LAND DISTRIBUTION AT SHILOH

¹ The entire Israelite community assembled at Shiloh and set up the tent of meeting there. The land had been subdued before them, ² but seven tribes among the Israelites were left who had not divided up their inheritance. ³ So Joshua asked the Israelites, "How long will you delay going out to take possession of the land that the LORD, the God of your ancestors, gave you? ⁴ Appoint for yourselves three men from each tribe, and I will send them out. They are to go and survey the land, write a description of it for the purpose of their inheritance, and return to me. ⁵ Then they are to divide it into seven portions. Judah is to remain in its territory in the south and Joseph's family in their territory in the north. ⁶ When you have written a description of the seven portions of land and brought it to me, I will cast lots for you here in the presence of the LORD our God. ⁷ But the Levites among you do not get a portion, because their inheritance is the priesthood of the LORD. Gad, Reuben, and half the tribe of Manasseh have taken their inheritance beyond the Jordan to the east, which Moses the LORD's servant gave them."

⁸ As the men prepared to go, Joshua commanded them to write down a description of the land, saying, "Go and survey the land, write a description of it, and return to me. I will then cast lots for you here in Shiloh in the presence of the LORD." ⁹ So the men left, went through the land, and described it by towns in a document of seven sections. They returned to Joshua at the camp in Shiloh. ¹⁰ Joshua cast lots for them at Shiloh in the presence of the LORD where he distributed the land to the Israelites according to their divisions.

BENJAMIN'S INHERITANCE

¹¹ The lot came up for the tribe of Benjamin's descendants by their clans, and their allotted territory lay between Judah's descendants and Joseph's descendants.

¹² Their border on the north side began at the Jordan, ascended to the slope of Jericho on the north, through the hill country westward, and ended at the wilderness

around Beth-aven. [13] From there the border went toward Luz, to the southern slope of Luz (that is, Bethel); it then went down by Ataroth-addar, over the hill south of Lower Beth-horon.

[14] On the west side, from the hill facing Beth-horon on the south, the border curved, turning southward, and ended at Kiriath-baal (that is, Kiriath-jearim), a city of the descendants of Judah. This was the west side of their border.

[15] The south side began at the edge of Kiriath-jearim, and the border extended westward; it went to the spring at the Waters of Nephtoah. [16] The border descended to the foot of the hill that faces Ben Hinnom Valley at the northern end of Rephaim Valley. It ran down Hinnom Valley toward the south Jebusite slope and downward to En-rogel. [17] It curved northward and went to En-shemesh and on to Geliloth, which is opposite the Ascent of Adummim, and continued down to the Stone of Bohan son of Reuben. [18] Then it went north to the slope opposite the Arabah and proceeded into the plains. [19] The border continued to the north slope of Beth-hoglah and ended at the northern bay of the Dead Sea, at the southern end of the Jordan. This was the southern border.

[20] The Jordan formed the border on the east side.

This was the inheritance of Benjamin's descendants, by their clans, according to its surrounding borders.

BENJAMIN'S CITIES

[21] These were the cities of the tribe of Benjamin's descendants by their clans:

Jericho, Beth-hoglah, Emek-keziz, [22] Beth-arabah, Zemaraim, Bethel, [23] Avvim, Parah, Ophrah, [24] Chephar-ammoni, Ophni, and Geba—twelve cities, with their settlements; [25] Gibeon, Ramah, Beeroth, [26] Mizpeh, Chephirah, Mozah, [27] Rekem, Irpeel, Taralah, [28] Zela, Haeleph, Jebus (that is, Jerusalem), Gibeah, and Kiriath—fourteen cities, with their settlements.

This was the inheritance for Benjamin's descendants by their clans.

Joshua 19
SIMEON'S INHERITANCE

[1] The second lot came out for Simeon, for the tribe of his descendants by their clans, but their inheritance was within the inheritance given to Judah's descendants. [2] Their inheritance included

Beer-sheba (or Sheba), Moladah, [3] Hazar-shual, Balah, Ezem, [4] Eltolad, Bethul, Hormah, [5] Ziklag, Beth-marcaboth, Hazar-susah, [6] Beth-lebaoth, and Sharuhen—thirteen cities, with their settlements; [7] Ain, Rimmon, Ether, and Ashan—four cities, with their settlements; [8] and all the settlements surrounding these cities as far as Baalath-beer (Ramah in the south).

This was the inheritance of the tribe of Simeon's descendants by their clans. [9] The inheritance of Simeon's descendants was within the territory of Judah's descendants, because the share for Judah's descendants was too large. So Simeon's descendants received an inheritance within Judah's portion.

ZEBULUN'S INHERITANCE

[10] The third lot came up for Zebulun's descendants by their clans.

The territory of their inheritance stretched as far as Sarid; [11] their border went up westward to Maralah, reached Dabbesheth, and met the brook east of Jokneam. [12] From Sarid, it turned due east along the border of Chisloth-tabor, went to Daberath, and went up to Japhia. [13] From there, it went due east to Gath-hepher and to Eth-kazin; it extended to Rimmon, curving around to Neah. [14] The border then circled around Neah on the north to Hannathon and ended at Iphtah-el Valley, [15] along with Kattath, Nahalal, Shimron, Idalah, and Bethlehem—twelve cities, with their settlements.

[16] This was the inheritance of Zebulun's descendants by their clans, these cities, with their settlements.

ISSACHAR'S INHERITANCE

[17] The fourth lot came out for the tribe of Issachar's descendants by their clans.

[18] Their territory went to Jezreel, and included Chesulloth, Shunem, [19] Hapharaim, Shion, Anaharath, [20] Rabbith, Kishion, Ebez, [21] Remeth, En-gannim, En-haddah, and Beth-pazzez. [22] The border reached Tabor, Shahazumah, and Beth-shemesh, and ended at the Jordan—sixteen cities, with their settlements.

[23] This was the inheritance of the tribe of Issachar's descendants by their clans, the cities, with their settlements.

ASHER'S INHERITANCE

[24] The fifth lot came out for the tribe of Asher's descendants by their clans.

[25] Their boundary included Helkath, Hali, Beten, Achshaph, [26] Allammelech, Amad, and Mishal and reached westward to Carmel and Shihor-libnath. [27] It turned eastward to Beth-dagon, reached Zebulun and Iphtah-el Valley, north toward Beth-emek and Neiel, and went north to Cabul, [28] Ebron, Rehob, Hammon, and Kanah, as far as greater Sidon. [29] The boundary then turned to Ramah as far as the fortified city of Tyre; it turned back to Hosah and ended at the Mediterranean Sea, including Mahalab, Achzib, [30] Ummah, Aphek, and Rehob—twenty-two cities, with their settlements.

[31] This was the inheritance of the tribe of Asher's descendants by their clans, these cities with their settlements.

NAPHTALI'S INHERITANCE

[32] The sixth lot came out for Naphtali's descendants by their clans.

[33] Their boundary went from Heleph and from the oak in Zaanannim, including Adami-nekeb and Jabneel, as far as Lakkum, and ended at the Jordan. [34] To the west, the boundary turned to Aznoth-tabor and went from there to Hukkok, reaching Zebulun on the south, Asher on the west, and Judah at the Jordan on the east. [35] The fortified cities were Ziddim, Zer, Hammath, Rakkath, Chinnereth, [36] Adamah, Ramah, Hazor, [37] Kedesh, Edrei, En-hazor, [38] Iron, Migdal-el, Horem, Beth-anath, and Beth-shemesh—nineteen cities, with their settlements.

[39] This was the inheritance of the tribe of Naphtali's descendants by their clans, the cities with their settlements.

DAN'S INHERITANCE

[40] The seventh lot came out for the tribe of Dan's descendants by their clans.

[41] The territory of their inheritance included Zorah, Eshtaol, Ir-shemesh, [42] Shaalabbin, Aijalon, Ithlah, [43] Elon, Timnah, Ekron, [44] Eltekeh, Gibbethon, Baalath, [45] Jehud, Bene-berak, Gath-rimmon, [46] Me-jarkon, and Rakkon, with the territory facing Joppa.

[47] When the territory of the descendants of Dan slipped out of their control, they went up and fought against Leshem, captured it, and struck it down with the sword. So they took possession of it, lived there, and renamed Leshem after their ancestor Dan. [48] This was the inheritance of the tribe of Dan's descendants by their clans, these cities with their settlements.

JOSHUA'S INHERITANCE

[49] When they had finished distributing the land into its territories, the Israelites gave Joshua son of Nun an inheritance among them. [50] By the LORD's command, they gave him the city Timnath-serah in the hill country of Ephraim, which he requested. He rebuilt the city and lived in it.

[51] These were the portions that the priest Eleazar, Joshua son of Nun, and the family heads distributed to the Israelite tribes by lot at Shiloh in the LORD's presence at the entrance to the tent of meeting. So they finished dividing up the land.

Acts 13:16–23

[16] Paul stood up and motioned with his hand and said, "Fellow Israelites, and you who fear God, listen! [17] The God of this people Israel chose our ancestors, made the people prosper during their stay in the land of Egypt, and led them out of it with a mighty arm. [18] And for about forty years he put up with them in the wilderness; [19] and after destroying seven nations in the land of Canaan, he gave them their land as an inheritance. [20] This all took about 450 years. After this, he gave them judges until Samuel the prophet. [21] Then

they asked for a king, and God gave them Saul the son of Kish, a man of the tribe of Benjamin, for forty years. ²² After removing him, he raised up David as their king and testified about him, 'I have found David the son of Jesse to be a man after my own heart, who will carry out all my will.'

²³ "From this man's descendants, as he promised, God brought to Israel the Savior, Jesus."

Romans 4:16–22

¹⁶ This is why the promise is by faith, so that it may be according to grace, to guarantee it to all the descendants—not only to the one who is of the law but also to the one who is of Abraham's faith. He is the father of us all. ¹⁷ As it is written: I have made you the father of many nations—in the presence of the God in whom he believed, the one who gives life to the dead and calls things into existence that do not exist. ¹⁸ He believed, hoping against hope, so that he became the father of many nations according to what had been spoken: So will your descendants be. ¹⁹ He did not weaken in faith when he considered his own body to be already dead (since he was about a hundred years old) and also the deadness of Sarah's womb. ²⁰ He did not waver in unbelief at God's promise but was strengthened in his faith and gave glory to God, ²¹ because he was fully convinced that what God had promised, he was also able to do. ²² Therefore, it was credited to him for righteousness.

The Lord Fulfills His Promises

DAY 23

Joshua 20
Joshua 21
Exodus 21:12–14
Hebrews 4:14–16

SEA OF GALILEE • NAPHTALI

(6) Joshua 20
CITIES OF REFUGE

¹ Then the LORD spoke to Joshua, ² "Tell the Israelites: Select your cities of refuge, as I instructed you through Moses, ³ so that a person who kills someone unintentionally or accidentally may flee there. These will be your refuge from the avenger of blood. ⁴ When someone flees to one of these cities, stands at the entrance of the city gate, and states his case before the elders of that city, they are to bring him into the city and give him a place to live among them. ⁵ And if the avenger of blood pursues him, they must not hand the one who committed manslaughter over to him, for he killed his neighbor accidentally and did not hate him beforehand. ⁶ He is to stay in that city until he stands trial before the assembly and until the death of the high priest serving at that time. Then the one who committed manslaughter may return home to his own city from which he fled."

⁷ So they designated Kedesh in the hill country of Naphtali in Galilee, Shechem in the hill country of Ephraim, and Kiriath-arba (that is, Hebron) in the hill country of Judah. ⁸ Across the Jordan east of Jericho, they selected Bezer on the wilderness plateau from Reuben's tribe, Ramoth in Gilead from Gad's tribe, and Golan in Bashan from Manasseh's tribe.

⁹ These are the cities appointed for all the Israelites and the aliens residing among them, so that anyone who kills a person unintentionally may flee there and not die at the hand of the avenger of blood until he stands before the assembly.

Joshua 21
CITIES OF THE LEVITES

¹ The Levite family heads approached the priest Eleazar, Joshua son of Nun, and the family heads of the Israelite tribes. ² At Shiloh, in the land of Canaan, they told them, "The LORD commanded through Moses that we be given cities to live in, with their pasturelands for our livestock." ³ So the Israelites, by the LORD's command, gave the Levites these cities with their pasturelands from their inheritance.

⁴ The lot came out for the Kohathite clans: The Levites who were the descendants of the priest Aaron received thirteen cities by lot from the tribes of Judah, Simeon, and Benjamin. ⁵ The remaining descendants of Kohath received ten cities by lot from the clans of the tribes of Ephraim, Dan, and half the tribe of Manasseh.

⁶ Gershon's descendants received thirteen cities by lot from the clans of the tribes of Issachar, Asher, Naphtali, and half the tribe of Manasseh in Bashan.

⁷ Merari's descendants received twelve cities for their clans from the tribes of Reuben, Gad, and Zebulun.

⁸ The Israelites gave these cities with their pasturelands around them to the Levites by lot, as the LORD had commanded through Moses.

CITIES OF AARON'S DESCENDANTS

⁹ The Israelites gave these cities by name from the tribes of the descendants of Judah and Simeon ¹⁰ to the descendants of Aaron from the Kohathite clans of the Levites, because they received the first lot. ¹¹ They gave them Kiriath-arba (that is, Hebron; Arba was the father of Anak) with its surrounding pasturelands in the hill country of Judah. ¹² But they gave the fields and settlements of the city to Caleb son of Jephunneh as his possession.

¹³ They gave to the descendants of the priest Aaron:

Hebron, the city of refuge for the one who commits manslaughter, with its pasturelands, Libnah with its pasturelands, ¹⁴ Jattir with its pasturelands, Eshtemoa with its pasturelands, ¹⁵ Holon with its pasturelands, Debir with its pasturelands, ¹⁶ Ain with its pasturelands, Juttah with its pasturelands, and Beth-shemesh with its pasturelands—nine cities from these two tribes.

¹⁷ From the tribe of Benjamin they gave:

Gibeon with its pasturelands, Geba with its pasturelands, ¹⁸ Anathoth with its pasturelands, and Almon with its pasturelands—four cities. ¹⁹ All thirteen cities with their pasturelands were for the priests, the descendants of Aaron.

[20] The allotted cities to the remaining clans of Kohath's descendants, who were Levites, came from the tribe of Ephraim. [21] The Israelites gave them:

Shechem, the city of refuge for the one who commits manslaughter, with its pasturelands in the hill country of Ephraim, Gezer with its pasturelands, [22] Kibzaim with its pasturelands, and Beth-horon with its pasturelands—four cities.

[23] From the tribe of Dan they gave:

Elteke with its pasturelands, Gibbethon with its pasturelands, [24] Aijalon with its pasturelands, and Gath-rimmon with its pasturelands—four cities.

[25] From half the tribe of Manasseh they gave:

Taanach with its pasturelands and Gath-rimmon with its pasturelands—two cities.

[26] All ten cities with their pasturelands were for the clans of Kohath's other descendants.

CITIES OF GERSHON'S DESCENDANTS

[27] From half the tribe of Manasseh, they gave to the descendants of Gershon, who were one of the Levite clans:

Golan, the city of refuge for the one who commits manslaughter, with its pasturelands in Bashan, and Beeshterah with its pasturelands—two cities.

[28] From the tribe of Issachar they gave:

Kishion with its pasturelands, Daberath with its pasturelands, [29] Jarmuth with its pasturelands, and En-gannim with its pasturelands—four cities.

[30] From the tribe of Asher they gave:

Mishal with its pasturelands, Abdon with its pasturelands, [31] Helkath with its pasturelands, and Rehob with its pasturelands—four cities.

[32] From the tribe of Naphtali they gave:

Kedesh in Galilee, the city of refuge for the one who commits manslaughter, with its pasturelands, Hammoth-dor with its pasturelands, and Kartan with its pasturelands—three cities.

[33] All thirteen cities with their pasturelands were for the Gershonites by their clans.

CITIES OF MERARI'S DESCENDANTS

[34] From the tribe of Zebulun, they gave to the clans of the descendants of Merari, who were the remaining Levites:

Jokneam with its pasturelands, Kartah with its pasturelands, [35] Dimnah with its pasturelands, and Nahalal with its pasturelands—four cities.

[36] From the tribe of Reuben they gave:

Bezer with its pasturelands, Jahzah with its pasturelands, [37] Kedemoth with its pasturelands, and Mephaath with its pasturelands—four cities.

[38] From the tribe of Gad they gave:

Ramoth in Gilead, the city of refuge for the one who commits manslaughter, with its pasturelands, Mahanaim with its pasturelands, [39] Heshbon with its pasturelands, and Jazer with its pasturelands—four cities in all. [40] All twelve cities were allotted to the clans of Merari's descendants, the remaining Levite clans.

[41] Within the Israelite possession there were forty-eight cities in all with their pasturelands for the Levites. [42] Each of these cities had its own surrounding pasturelands; this was true for all the cities.

THE LORD'S PROMISES FULFILLED

[43] So the LORD gave Israel all the land he had sworn to give their ancestors, and they took possession of it and settled there.

⁴⁴ The LORD gave them rest on every side according to all he had sworn to their ancestors.

None of their enemies were able to stand against them, for the LORD handed over all their enemies to them. ⁴⁵ None of the good promises the LORD had made to the house of Israel failed. Everything was fulfilled.

Exodus 21:12–14
LAWS ABOUT PERSONAL INJURY

¹² "Whoever strikes a person so that he dies must be put to death. ¹³ But if he did not intend any harm, and yet God allowed it to happen, I will appoint a place for you where he may flee. ¹⁴ If a person schemes and willfully acts against his neighbor to murder him, you must take him from my altar to be put to death."

Hebrews 4:14–16
OUR GREAT HIGH PRIEST

¹⁴ Therefore, since we have a great high priest who has passed through the heavens—Jesus the Son of God—let us hold fast to our confession. ¹⁵ For we do not have a high priest who is unable to sympathize with our weaknesses, but one who has been tempted in every way as we are, yet without sin. ¹⁶ Therefore, let us approach the throne of grace with boldness, so that we may receive mercy and find grace to help us in time of need.

NOTES

JOSHUA

&

JESUS

Throughout the Old Testament, the lives of many men and women point ahead to Jesus Christ. Joshua not only bears the same Hebrew name as Jesus (*Yeshua*, translated as "Yahweh saves"), but his life also offers us a glimpse of the complete and lasting victory to come in Christ. Here are some of the parallels between the lives of Joshua and Jesus.

Joshua led the people of God in battle against physical enemies.

JOS 1:1-5; 8:1-2

Joshua led God's people to their inheritance in the promised land.

JOS 1:6

Joshua carried out the law given to him by Moses.

JOS 1:7-8

Jesus battles spiritual enemies on behalf of the people of God.

MT 8:28-32
JN 8:31-36

Jesus provides the only way to our inheritance of eternal life.

EPH 1:11-13, 18-19

Jesus fulfilled the law.

MT 5:17-20
RM 10:4

Joshua crossed
the Jordan riverbed
on foot.

JOS 3:7-17

Joshua appointed
twelve men to
represent God's people
as the twelve tribes
of Israel.

JOS 4:1-7

Joshua experienced
miracles, such as
seeing the walls of
Jericho fall.

JOS 6:1-5, 20

Joshua brought
Rahab and her family
into the family of God
when they trusted
the Lord.

JOS 6:22-23

Jesus walked on the
Sea of Galilee.

MT 14:22-33

Jesus appointed the
twelve disciples to
spread the news about
the Son of God.

MK 3:13-19

Jesus performed
miracles, such as
turning water into
wine.

JN 2:1-11

Jesus brings sinners
who trust in Him into
the family of God.

JN 3:16-17

Joshua fought
battles using
physical weapons.

JOS 8:18-19, 24-26

Joshua led the people
of God into temporary,
physical rest from
their enemies.

JOS 21:44; 22:4

Joshua brought
physical victory.

JOS 24:11-13

Joshua sought
covenant renewal.

JOS 24:14-28

Jesus wins battles
using spiritual
weapons.

MT 4:1-11

Jesus guarantees
the people of God
eternal rest from
their enemies.

HEB 4:1-11

Jesus brings
spiritual victory.

MT 27:50-53
RM 8:1-4

Jesus fulfilled the
old covenant and
established the
new covenant.

HEB 9:11-28

An Altar of Witness

Joshua 22

EASTERN TRIBES RETURN HOME

¹ Joshua summoned the Reubenites, Gadites, and half the tribe of Manasseh ² and told them, "You have done everything Moses the LORD's servant commanded you and have obeyed me in everything I commanded you. ³ You have not deserted your brothers even once this whole time but have carried out the requirement of the command of the LORD your God. ⁴ Now that he has given your brothers rest, just as he promised them, return to your homes in your own land that Moses the LORD's servant gave you across the Jordan. ⁵ Only carefully obey the command and instruction that Moses the LORD's servant gave you: to love the LORD your God, walk in all his ways, keep his commands, be loyal to him, and serve him with all your heart and all your soul."

⁶ Joshua blessed them and sent them on their way, and they went to their homes. ⁷ Moses had given territory to half the tribe of Manasseh in Bashan, but Joshua had given territory to the other half, with their brothers, on the west side of the Jordan. When Joshua sent them to their homes and blessed

them, ⁸ he said, "Return to your homes with great wealth: a huge number of cattle, and silver, gold, bronze, iron, and a large quantity of clothing. Share the spoil of your enemies with your brothers."

EASTERN TRIBES BUILD AN ALTAR

⁹ The Reubenites, Gadites, and half the tribe of Manasseh left the Israelites at Shiloh in the land of Canaan to return to their own land of Gilead, which they took possession of according to the LORD's command through Moses. ¹⁰ When they came to the region of the Jordan in the land of Canaan, the Reubenites, Gadites, and half the tribe of Manasseh built a large, impressive altar there by the Jordan.

¹¹ Then the Israelites heard it said, "Look, the Reubenites, Gadites, and half the tribe of Manasseh have built an altar on the frontier of the land of Canaan at the region of the Jordan, on the Israelite side." ¹² When the Israelites heard this, the

entire Israelite community assembled at Shiloh to go to war against them.

EXPLANATION OF THE ALTAR

[13] The Israelites sent Phinehas son of Eleazar the priest to the Reubenites, Gadites, and half the tribe of Manasseh, in the land of Gilead. [14] They sent ten leaders with him—one family leader for each tribe of Israel. All of them were heads of their ancestral families among the clans of Israel. [15] They went to the Reubenites, Gadites, and half the tribe of Manasseh, in the land of Gilead, and told them, [16] "This is what the LORD's entire community says: 'What is this treachery you have committed today against the God of Israel by turning away from the LORD and building an altar for yourselves, so that you are in rebellion against the LORD today? [17] Wasn't the iniquity of Peor, which brought a plague on the LORD's community, enough for us? We have not cleansed ourselves from it even to this day, [18] and now would you turn away from the LORD? If you rebel against the LORD today, tomorrow he will be angry with the entire community of Israel. [19] But if the land you possess is defiled, cross over to the land the LORD possesses where the LORD's tabernacle stands, and take possession of it among us. But don't rebel against the LORD or against us by building for yourselves an altar other than the altar of the LORD our God. [20] Wasn't Achan son of Zerah unfaithful regarding what was set apart for destruction, bringing wrath on the entire community of Israel? He was not the only one who perished because of his iniquity.'"

[21] The Reubenites, Gadites, and half the tribe of Manasseh answered the heads of the Israelite clans, [22] "The Mighty One, God, the LORD! The Mighty One, God, the LORD! He knows, and may Israel also know. Do not spare us today, if it was in rebellion or treachery against the LORD [23] that we have built for ourselves an altar to turn away from him. May the LORD himself hold us accountable if we intended to offer burnt offerings and grain offerings on it, or to sacrifice fellowship offerings on it. [24] We actually did this from a specific concern that in the future your descendants might say to our descendants, 'What relationship do you have with the LORD, the God of Israel? [25] For the LORD has made the Jordan a border between us and you descendants of Reuben and Gad.

You have no share in the LORD!' So your descendants may cause our descendants to stop fearing the LORD.

[26] "Therefore we said: Let's take action and build an altar for ourselves, but not for burnt offering or sacrifice. [27] Instead, it is to be a witness between us and you, and between the generations after us, so that we may carry out the worship of the LORD in his presence with our burnt offerings, sacrifices, and fellowship offerings. Then in the future, your descendants will not be able to say to our descendants, 'You have no share in the LORD!' [28] We thought that if they said this to us or to our generations in the future, we would reply: Look at the replica of the LORD's altar that our ancestors made, not for burnt offering or sacrifice, but as a witness between us and you. [29] We would never ever rebel against the LORD or turn away from him today by building an altar for burnt offering, grain offering, or sacrifice, other than the altar of the LORD our God, which is in front of his tabernacle."

CONFLICT RESOLVED

[30] When the priest Phinehas and the community leaders, the heads of Israel's clans who were with him, heard what the descendants of Reuben, Gad, and Manasseh had to say, they were pleased. [31] Phinehas son of Eleazar the priest said to the descendants of Reuben, Gad, and Manasseh,

> "Today we know that the LORD is among us,

because you have not committed this treachery against him. As a result, you have rescued the Israelites from the LORD's power."

[32] Then the priest Phinehas son of Eleazar and the leaders returned from the Reubenites and Gadites in the land of Gilead to the Israelites in the land of Canaan and brought back a report to them. [33] The Israelites were pleased with the report, and they blessed God. They spoke no more about going to war against them to ravage the land where the Reubenites and Gadites lived. [34] So the Reubenites and Gadites named the altar: It is a witness between us that the LORD is God.

Psalm 7:8–10

8 The LORD judges the peoples;
vindicate me, LORD,
according to my righteousness and my integrity.

9 Let the evil of the wicked come to an end,
but establish the righteous.
The one who examines the thoughts and emotions
is a righteous God.
10 My shield is with God,
who saves the upright in heart.

2 Corinthians 1:21–22

21 Now it is God who strengthens us together with you in Christ, and who has anointed us. 22 He has also put his seal on us and given us the Spirit in our hearts as a down payment.

You know with all your heart and all your soul that none of the
good promises the LORD your God made to you has failed.

JOSHUA 23:14

Joshua's Farewell Address

Joshua 23
JOSHUA'S FAREWELL ADDRESS

¹ A long time after the LORD had given Israel rest from all the enemies around them, Joshua was old, advanced in age. ² So Joshua summoned all Israel, including its elders, leaders, judges, and officers, and said to them, "I am old, advanced in age, ³ and you have seen for yourselves everything the LORD your God did to all these nations on your account, because it was the LORD your God who was fighting for you. ⁴ See, I have allotted these remaining nations to you as an inheritance for your tribes, including all the nations I have destroyed, from the Jordan westward to the Mediterranean Sea. ⁵ The LORD your God will force them back on your account and drive them out before you so that you can take possession of their land, as the LORD your God promised you.

⁶ "Be very strong and continue obeying all that is written in the book of the law of Moses, so that you do not turn from it to the right or left ⁷ and

so that you do not associate with these nations remaining among you. Do not call on the names of their gods or make an oath to them; do not serve them or bow in worship to them. [8] Instead, be loyal to the LORD your God, as you have been to this day.

[9] "The LORD has driven out great and powerful nations before you, and no one is able to stand against you to this day. [10] One of you routed a thousand because the LORD your God was fighting for you, as he promised. [11] So diligently watch yourselves! Love the LORD your God! [12] If you ever turn away and become loyal to the rest of these nations remaining among you, and if you intermarry or associate with them and they with you, [13] know for certain that the LORD your God will not continue to drive these nations out before you. They will become a snare and a trap for you, a sharp stick for your sides and thorns in your eyes, until you disappear from this good land the LORD your God has given you.

[14] "I am now going the way of the whole earth, and you know with all your heart and all your soul that none of the good promises the LORD your God made to you has failed. Everything was fulfilled for you; not one promise has failed. [15] Since every good thing the LORD your God promised you has come about, so he will bring on you every bad thing until he has annihilated you from this good land the LORD your God has given you. [16] If you break the covenant of the LORD your God, which he commanded you, and go and serve other gods, and bow in worship to them, the LORD's anger will burn against you, and you will quickly disappear from this good land he has given you."

Matthew 22:37–40
[37] He said to him,

"Love the Lord your God with all your heart, with all your soul, and with all your mind.

[38] This is the greatest and most important command. [39] The second is like it: Love your neighbor as yourself. [40] All the Law and the Prophets depend on these two commands."

Philippians 1:6
I am sure of this, that he who started a good work in you will carry it on to completion until the day of Christ Jesus.

DATE

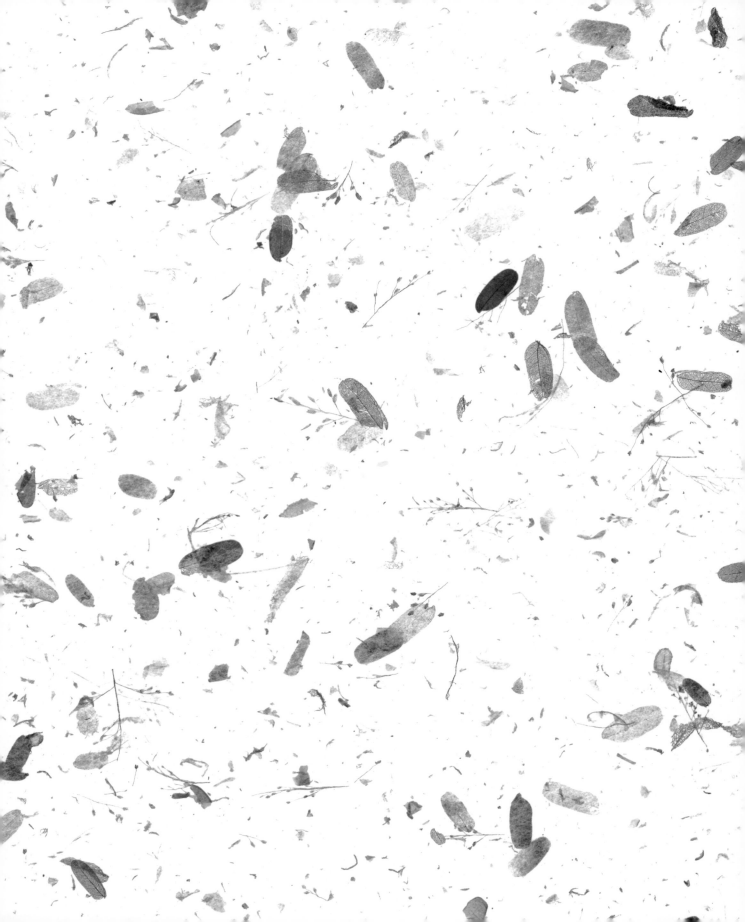

Israel Renews Their Covenant Commitment

Joshua 24
REVIEW OF ISRAEL'S HISTORY

¹ Joshua assembled all the tribes of Israel at Shechem and summoned Israel's elders, leaders, judges, and officers, and they presented themselves before God. ² Joshua said to all the people, "This is what the LORD, the God of Israel, says: 'Long ago your ancestors, including Terah, the father of Abraham and Nahor, lived beyond the Euphrates River and worshiped other gods. ³ But I took your father Abraham from the region beyond the Euphrates River, led him throughout the land of Canaan, and multiplied his descendants. I gave him Isaac, ⁴ and to Isaac I gave Jacob and Esau. I gave the hill country of Seir to Esau as a possession.

"'Jacob and his sons, however, went down to Egypt. ⁵ I sent Moses and Aaron, and I defeated Egypt by what I did within it, and afterward I brought you out. ⁶ When I brought your ancestors out of Egypt and you reached the Red Sea, the Egyptians pursued your ancestors with chariots and horsemen as far as the sea. ⁷ Your ancestors cried out to the LORD, so he put darkness between you and the Egyptians, and brought the sea over them, engulfing them. Your own eyes saw what I did to Egypt. After that, you lived in the wilderness a long time.

⁸ "'Later, I brought you to the land of the Amorites who lived beyond the Jordan. They fought against you, but I handed them over to you. You possessed their land, and I annihilated them before you. ⁹ Balak son of Zippor, king of Moab, set out to fight against Israel. He sent for Balaam son of Beor to curse you, ¹⁰ but I would not listen to Balaam. Instead, he repeatedly blessed you, and I rescued you from him.

11 "'You then crossed the Jordan and came to Jericho. Jericho's citizens—as well as the Amorites, Perizzites, Canaanites, Hethites, Girgashites, Hivites, and Jebusites—fought against you, but I handed them over to you. 12 I sent hornets ahead of you, and they drove out the two Amorite kings before you. It was not by your sword or bow. 13 I gave you a land you did not labor for, and cities you did not build, though you live in them; you are eating from vineyards and olive groves you did not plant.'

⑧ THE COVENANT RENEWAL

14 "Therefore, fear the LORD and worship him in sincerity and truth. Get rid of the gods your ancestors worshiped beyond the Euphrates River and in Egypt, and worship the LORD. 15 But if it doesn't please you to worship the LORD, choose for yourselves today: Which will you worship—the gods your ancestors worshiped beyond the Euphrates River or the gods of the Amorites in whose land you are living? As for me and my family, we will worship the LORD."

16 The people replied, "We will certainly not abandon the LORD to worship other gods! 17 For the LORD our God brought us and our ancestors out of the land of Egypt, out of the place of slavery, and performed these great signs before our eyes. He also protected us all along the way we went and among all the peoples whose lands we traveled through. 18 The LORD drove out before us all the peoples, including the Amorites who lived in the land. We too will worship the LORD, because he is our God."

19 But Joshua told the people, "You will not be able to worship the LORD, because he is a holy God. He is a jealous God; he will not forgive your transgressions and sins. 20 If you abandon the LORD and worship foreign gods, he will turn against you, harm you, and completely destroy you, after he has been good to you."

21 "No!" the people answered Joshua. "We will worship the LORD."

22 Joshua then told the people, "You are witnesses against yourselves that you yourselves have chosen to worship the LORD."

"We are witnesses," they said.

23 "Then get rid of the foreign gods that are among you and turn your hearts to the LORD, the God of Israel."

24 So the people said to Joshua, "We will worship the LORD our God and obey him."

25 On that day Joshua made a covenant for the people at Shechem and established a statute and ordinance for them. 26 Joshua recorded these things in the book of the law of God; he also took a large stone and set it up there under the oak at the sanctuary of the LORD. 27 And Joshua said to all the people, "You see this stone—it will be a witness against us, for it has heard all the words the LORD said to us, and it will be a witness against you, so that you will not deny your God." 28 Then Joshua sent the people away, each to his own inheritance.

BURIAL OF THREE LEADERS

29 After these things, the LORD's servant, Joshua son of Nun, died at the age of 110. 30 They buried him in his allotted territory at Timnath-serah, in the hill country of Ephraim north of Mount Gaash. 31 Israel worshiped the LORD throughout Joshua's lifetime and during the lifetimes of the elders who outlived Joshua and who had experienced all the works the LORD had done for Israel.

32 Joseph's bones, which the Israelites had brought up from Egypt, were buried at Shechem in the parcel of land Jacob had purchased from the sons of Hamor, Shechem's father, for a hundred pieces of silver. It was an inheritance for Joseph's descendants.

33 And Eleazar son of Aaron died, and they buried him at Gibeah, which had been given to his son Phinehas in the hill country of Ephraim.

Deuteronomy 7:9

Know that the LORD your God is God, the faithful God who keeps his gracious covenant loyalty for a thousand generations with those who love him and keep his commands.

Romans 8:28

We know that all things work together for the good of those who love God, who are called according to his purpose.

DATE

REFLECT & REMEMBER

In Joshua, stones or stone altars were often used to mark places where God's presence was evident or to memorialize fulfilled promises. Joshua 4 includes a detailed account of how the use of memorial stones helped God's people remember His faithfulness. We, too, are called to remember and proclaim God's work in our lives (2Pt 1:12).

I am sure of this, that he who started a good work in you will carry it on to completion until the day of Christ Jesus.

PHILIPPIANS 1:6

Reflect on all God has done for you and say a prayer of thankfulness. In the journaling space provided, write about how you might recommit to following God in the days ahead. Let this written account be your personal stone of remembrance to mark God's work in your life as you anticipate the work He will continue to do.

DAY 27: GRACE DAY

*Take this day to catch up on
your reading, pray, and rest in
the presence of the Lord.*

"Love the Lord your God with all your heart, with all your soul, and with all your mind."

MATTHEW 22:37

WEEKLY

DAY 28

Scripture is God-breathed and true. When we memorize it, we carry His Word with us wherever we go.

Throughout this reading plan, we've memorized Joshua 1:9. Take time this week to say the entire verse at once, and ask a friend or family member to test your memorization by having you say it to them. Call this verse to mind when you need to remember and proclaim God's promised faithfulness.

"Haven't I commanded you: be strong and courageous?

Do not be afraid or discouraged,

for the LORD your God is with you wherever you go."

JOSHUA 1:9

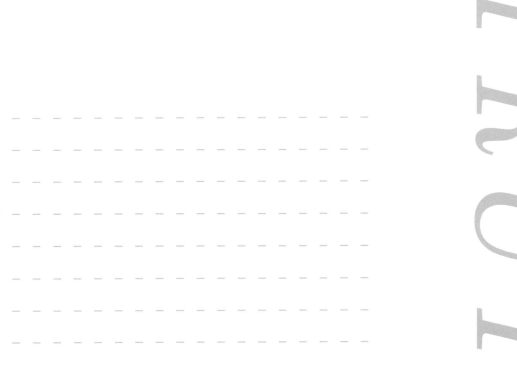

BENEDI

You know with all your heart
and all your soul that none of
the good promises the LORD
your God made to you has failed.

JOSHUA 23:14

CTION

CSB BOOK ABBREVIATIONS

BIBLIOGRAPHY

Barry, John D., et. al., eds. "Introduction to Joshua." In *Faithlife Study Bible*. Bellingham: Lexham Press, 2016.

Easton, M. G. "Joshua." In *Easton's Bible Dictionary*. New York: Harper & Brothers, 1893.

FRIEND, WE'VE BEEN THERE...

Reading the Bible can be hard. In a world of so many distractions, constant notifications, and endless to-dos, it's easy to slip into a rut when it comes to reading God's Word.

Let's get unstuck! Be a woman in the Word every day with the She Reads Truth Subscription Box. For just $20 a month, you'll get each brand new Study Book we create delivered right to your door, plus exclusive perks like free gifts, early access to sales, and more! Our monthly delivery service sets you up to engage with God's Word on the good days, the bad days, and all the days in between. We'll do the planning for you so all you have to do is show up, open God's Word, and then do it again tomorrow.

USE CODE SUB20 FOR 20% OFF

YOUR FIRST MONTH'S BOX!

SUBSCRIPTION.SHOPSHEREADSTRUTH.COM

WHERE DID I STUDY?

O HOME
O OFFICE
O COFFEE SHOP
O CHURCH
O A FRIEND'S HOUSE
O OTHER:

WHAT WAS I LISTENING TO?

ARTIST:

SONG:

PLAYLIST:

WHEN DID I STUDY?

O MORNING
O AFTERNOON
O NIGHT

HOW DID I FIND DELIGHT IN GOD'S WORD?

WHAT WAS HAPPENING IN MY LIFE?

WHAT WAS HAPPENING IN THE WORLD?

MONTH	DAY	YEAR

END DATE